ROOKIE
ON LOVE

45 VOICES ON ROMANCE, FRIENDSHIP, AND SELF-CARE

EDITED BY TAVI GEVINSON

Teen
302
Gevinson

Editor: Tavi Gevinson
Publisher: Lauren Redding
Lead Story Editor: Tina Lee
Lead Artist and Cover Designer: Allegra Lockstadt
Poetry Editor: Diamond Sharp
Designers: Kristin Boyle, Maggie Edkins

razorbill

An Imprint of Penguin Random House LLC
Penguin.com

First published in the United States of America by Razorbill, an imprint of Penguin
Random House LLC, 2018

LIBRARY OF CONGRESS CATALOGING-IN-PUBLICATION DATA IS AVAILABLE

ISBN: 9780448493992

Printed in the United States of America

1 3 5 7 9 10 8 6 4 2

CONTENTS

INTRODUCTION

Rookie is an online magazine made by and for teenagers and their cohorts of any age. I founded it in 2011, when I was a sophomore in high school, because I couldn't find a teen magazine that respected its readers' intelligence and had actual teens writing for it. In the time since, *Rookie* readers have made themselves known through our online community, at live events, and by starting their own zines, blogs, bands, clubs, and other manifestations of their creativity and brilliance. We'd always hoped to commemorate the magic all our contributors had made for RookieMag.com, so we published four anthologies—one for each year of high school—known as the *Rookie Yearbooks*. But we wanted to keep going, and we wanted to commission and publish new work that *wouldn't* live anywhere else, not even on the internet. We wanted to focus on a single subject, rather than a period of time. We wanted to see the variety of ways in which *Rookie* writers and artists, *Rookie* heroes we dreamed of working with, and *Rookie* readers who are on their way to becoming all of the above, would respond to the same prompt. We wanted a subject that would be totes chill, v. simple, and easy to understand. So we went with Love.

Behold: the next iteration of *Rookie* in print, featuring all-new essays, comics, and poetry by teens of all ages. Initially, I thought we'd commission pieces to check the box for every possible manifestation of this mysterious emotion: crushes, unrequited love, long-term, short-lived, long-distance, hookups, breakups, et cetera. Maybe we'd sequence them according to the timeline of a stereotypical relationship, from attraction to union to separation. The verdict would be in, *finally*. The meaning of love, captured in these pages.

But like anything worth doing or feeling, love is impossible to explain. Like anything in real life and not a book or movie or "Love Story" by Taylor Swift or "Love Story" by Mariah Carey or "Love Story (You and Me)" by Randy Newman, love doesn't always unfold according to a narrative structure. Plus, ending the book with a bunch of breakups felt bleak. What about the next part, where you find how great it is to be alone? And the part after that, where you meet someone else and create something new with them? Or where you choose to not be in a romantic relationship, or casually date, or have sex with whomever you want? Also, what about the love that persists all around us regardless of what we do or don't have going on romantically? The love you feel when working on something that really lights you up, or taking in a piece of art that seems to read your mind, or discovering a really good book (cough, fart)? The people who make your life feel so full that "The One" might actually be a multi-headed mutant? What about those days where you're just like, *I can't believe that I'm not only* not *depressed out of my mind, but that I also actually feel . . . in love with the world around me?!!?!* Or when you're like, "Whenever I get gloomy with the state of the world, I think about the arrivals gate at Heathrow Airport. General opinion's starting to make out that we live in a world of hatred and greed, but I don't see that. [. . .] If you look for it, I've got a sneaky feeling you'll find that love actually is all around."

OK, that was Hugh Grant's monologue from the beginning of *Love Actually*, but sometimes trying to write about love makes you sound like that!! And honestly, the thesis of that movie, however cheesy, is not *wrong*; if anything, the rest of the script falls short of that expansive claim. Love *is* all around, but its holding place is not always another person. Sometimes you find the best companion in yourself, or the fun of worshipping a teen idol, or the challenge of trying to understand love in its various forms. Just that *attempt*. The curiosity.

That's how I felt, working on this book. And, coming to its end, I feel pretty satisfied with the idea that love is a force that takes different forms, that can be more present in the feeling of writing than in a relationship, in memories or fantasies, in a conversation with an internet friend, in the way your dog waits for you to come home.

So, I am proposing a sequel to *Love Actually*, called *Love Actually—No, But Actually*, where everyone plays someone from *Rookie on Love*: Emma Thompson as Florence Welch's songwriting process (pg. 155), Bill Nighy as the beauty standards Alessia Cara calls into question (pg. 175), Chiwetel Ejiofor as Emma Straub's favorite books (pg. 57), Keira Knightley as the lion in Etgar Keret's short story (pg. 13), Colin Firth as Mitski Miyawaki's musical career (pg. 83), Liam Neeson as Marlo Thomas's acting coach (pg. 167), Laura Linney as Montgomery Clift in Hilton Als's tribute to the screen icon (pg. 191), January Jones as the love letters that taught Janet Mock she was a writer (pg. 3), Alan Rickman as the Gchat about YA romance between John Green and Rainbow Rowell (pg. 61), Rowan Atkinson as Gabourey Sidibe's self-described "Ho Phase" (pg. 67) . . . I mean, what a cast! No *wonder* it's a classic!

Prepare to be blown away by the poetry by Rookie readers, interviews and conversations, how-to's and direct advice, lyrical essays and timelines, and more questions than answers. I remain bowled over by every contribution, the sheer creativity and range in these interpretations of the most-written-about subject ever. Of course, though. That's what you get when you're just like: "I love your writing. Will you write about something that you love, too?"

And if anyone wants to produce a super-convoluted sequel to a beloved rom-com Christmas movie and obscure the moneymaking faces of at least ten international movie stars with giant objects-as-costumes, as in a school play, please get in touch!

Love (I say it in every Editor's Letter but now I extra-mean it),
Tavi

POSTCARDS FROM APOLLO 6

By Lena Blackmon

your hand rests on the waist of my sunflower sundress.
we waltz in a physics classroom.
there is sunlight inside of us:
it makes us graceful,
(as we tend to be, with our planetary bodies and gravitational
attraction)
kepler. and then the acceleration
away from each other.
drifting apart, but not in a
catastrophic way. like if apollo 6 floated down
instead of crashed.

HOW TO DEAL WITH REJECTION

*The writer and activist on getting over a crush
and into yourself.*

By Janet Mock

*I am a hopeless teenager who currently has a crush on a really cute boy
who is sitting next to me, and I want to get over him because I know
that he doesn't like me. Any suggestions, please?*

—*Riya, 18, New York City*

The first boy I ever loved lived two houses away from me. I have never pined for someone as deeply as I pined for Nathan. I stared at that boy so much I could've counted the number of freckles on his damn face. I watched him with an overwhelming lovesickness as he paraded pretty girl after pretty girl down our block. He'd wrap his tan, muscular arms around their shoulders, kiss their bronze necks, make them giggle.

I fantasized about being the kind of girl Nathan* would choose: a girl with silky long hair rather than one with a curly fro; a girl with breasts that bounced rather than one who wore a padded bra; a girl whose girlhood was never in question like mine was as a trans girl. But no matter how much I fantasized, I could not change that indisputable truth that Nathan did not like me back.

For so long, I blamed it on what I lacked, on what I was not. I am not saying this is what you are doing, but this is what

* Name has been changed.

3

my 14-year-old self did. I tried my best not to compare myself to Nathan's bevy of beauties, but I couldn't help it. Seeing them made it abundantly clear: they were chosen, and I was not. But that constant comparison only got in the way of me being able to see *myself* and appreciate what I had to offer. Just because Nathan— who I crushed on so damn *hard*—didn't want me, did not desire me, did not choose me, did not mean that I was not worthy of being chosen and being able to choose.

Still, grappling with that first rejection from the first boy I ever coveted broke my heart. I coped by writing love letters to him. I never sent them. (Oh goddess, I would have been mortified for him to *read* them!) But the act of writing those letters allowed me to sit down with myself and tell the truth about my feelings— those letters held me accountable to myself. They were initially addressed to him, but they always centered me. They centered me in ways that I wished he had centered me.

Eventually, I ran out of things to say to Nathan. But I realized I still had things to say, and I kept writing. I wrote about the things I wanted to do, to see, to experience. I wrote about my frustrations, desires, and, yes, new crushes. The letters were no longer addressed to Nathan; they actually stopped being letters and became my first journal, the roots of my journey as a writer. Those love-letters-turned-journal gave me the audacity to say what I wanted.

Centering myself, shifting the focus from my unattainable crush to my appreciation for what I had, who I was, and what I wanted, helped me get over him and get into me.

FWD: LETTER TO LEYB

We travel through screens, bodies, and text to our selves.

By Tova Benjamin

Rather than beginning this letter the usual way—by telling you where I am—I'm going to tell you about my medium (which will tell you where I am): the big screen of the library computer and the clunky keyboard with a different kind of grab. The mouse as its own entity, requiring me to cup it with my hand when I want to navigate my document, asking for more pressure from fingers, which click instead of press. I absentmindedly move the physical mouse around the library desk as I try to move the cursor down the screen. Behind the screen are two outlets. Underneath the screen is the computer itself.

Maybe I've broken our unspoken code by mentioning the computer, as we keep calling these emails to each other "letters." The most fascinating part of this Text and Digital Media class I'm taking has been discussions re: the materiality of the texts we read online. Not just in relation to legitimacy, or authority, but the very physicality—the plastic (?) my fingers cup now, the glass or fiberglass (?) of the screen, the wires that connect the screen to the wall behind me, which are then connected to a whole other slew of wires and hardware and fiberglass. Though we tend to think of media as existing in the faraway Cloud, it must be accessed through some physical medium. It does not exist untethered, floating in the air like thought.

> "[D]igital texts can seem strangely immaterial or disembodied. Like so much online, they are often

thought of as 'virtual' because they are so elusive as physical objects. No Web page would exist without a vast clutter of tangible stuff—the monitor on which it appears, but also the server computer, the client computer, the Internet 'backbone,' cables, routers, and switch hotels—but it is nonetheless strikingly intangible. What is it? Where is it?"

—Lisa Gitelman, *Always Already New*

(It is no coincidence that I am thinking about you as I read these writings—the person I began to love through a screen, or a digital text. Sometimes I consider the <body> of the person I got to know as I read your first letters, as you emailed them to me, text in your chosen font that appeared in other fonts when I opened your documents on my screen, words that shrank as I read your missives on my phone. It is strange to think about the materiality of *you* when we first met, and still now, as you largely exist in words— whether written, or spoken out loud.)

Later: Gitelman talks about the historicity of the internet, or the kind of history-making possible online. When I search for a web page, the results I receive are not the web page as it has existed in all its five to ten years or so, it's only the most recent version. The internet is just as good at covering up its history as it is at storing information. If I want to know what Facebook looked like seven years ago, I can go to another website and see screenshots other people took of their own Facebook pages seven years ago. But I can't get this kind of information from the Facebook.com page itself, which will only show me how it looks today, this moment, this second. A page that will already change in an hour when I check it again. Hence, the book's title: *Always Already New*.

(I am suddenly remembering how, on the phone a few nights ago, you told me—in a voice that was tenuous and tender and so self-aware that the tone was almost unrecognizable to me—you said, "But in some ways, Tova, I am just getting to know you." It is hard to separate you just now or still or always getting to know me [and vice versa] from the medium through which we are constantly engaging. The fact that every day we reach out and try to touch each other through the material wires and screens and keyboards of these digital texts and words that are constantly rewriting themselves and their own histories. But the digital conversations we had tumbled so effortlessly into our real-time interactions. The data that flowed between the time when I had not felt your body in my arms and the time when I did was continuous and never discrete, existing on an infinite plane of possibilities.

(When I see you now, I see your clean-shaven face, hear your words as they exist today, the person you are right now. But when I call you by your name you are not just the boy who has already newly rewritten himself but you are also a hard drive of data that I can access, data of all your past selves, the same selves that make up my experience as well.)

Deeper into Gitelman: Did you know that in 1996, the average lifespan of a web page was 75 days? That means in 1996 a single web page could only remain as it was for 75 days before someone would change it or move it or delete it. In 2000 the number was even smaller: 44 days. "Lifespan" as though a web page were a thing like a plant or a butterfly that flits for a few days and back before it becomes dust. But when a web page dies it becomes an error 404 page. After reading the lifespan number of 44 days, I searched for some old websites from the '90s, defunct sites like little graves, scattered across the Google search results. I typed, "How long is the average relationship?" Google tells me, in 0.63 seconds, that the average relationship lasts two years and nine months. This is the top search result, so it shows up in a little box, with a link to Katy Winter's 2014 *Daily Mail* article "Death of the Seven Year Itch," announcing, "The average relationship is just two years and nine months . . . and social media is to blame." The research was based on a survey of 1,953 UK adults. And now I've given this statistic a new lifespan, writing it to you.

Recently I read about all the effort put into keeping some endangered species alive—and I can't remember which—only to have it die a very short period later. I remember how heartbroken I felt when I read that. It isn't surprising to me that I would remember feeling heartbroken yet forget the name of the species, as though the feelings moving through my body are disconnected from the objects that caused them. As though feelings, like digital texts, have a strikingly intangible material life, the kinds of things that constantly rewrite themselves even as they exist in a trembling hard drive, vulnerable to damage and erasure and censorship. Sometimes I think, *I will never forget that I felt this way.* And then I do. It seems horribly scary to invest so much time and energy and emotion into something that will eventually wind down to the end of its life, be it 44 days or two years and nine months. And then what?

The last thing I read today was an essay about the digital and the analog by John Lavagnino and so much of it read like poetry to me. He talked about how the brain can or can't be compared to the computer, and whether the brain functions like digital (integers, or something that can be reduced to numbers) or like analog (data represented by physical quantities, which change continuously) or both. He writes that people tend to think of data as either digital or analog, but the essential nature of data is neither of these things; "digital" and "analog" are just systems, or ways of delivering data, and not the information itself. Still, at the same time, data isn't an independent entity—it's embedded in the systems that deliver it. I guess this is something like language. We sometimes think of language as divided into "body language" or "spoken language," body perhaps being the more subtle delivery, with spoken the more precise. But language isn't only "spoken" or "body"—the mouth or the gesture is just the *way* we deliver the communication. Like data, spoken language could be more subtle or less precise than body language, though we still think of communication as tied up with the systems (the hand, or the mouth) that transmit it. Probably because language can't be entirely separated from these systems, it is hard to communicate language without my body, or my mouth.

(Remember the first "I love you" that you sent me? And the many times you've said or sent it since, which have all been mediated by some type of technology? When you sent that first "I love you" it upset me, because I thought it wasn't *real*, and I told you that I wouldn't believe you—couldn't believe you loved me—until you told me in person. But the words "I love you," and the feelings behind them, aren't the systems that deliver them. Even though your "I love you" was transmitted digitally, in a text message, prefaced by the code that sent it, a compressed combination of numbers and symbols—even so, the message itself is unchanged. In this sense, "I love you" is both quantitative and infinite, a set of signifiers that hold the same network of feelings whether you deliver it to me digitally, or write it on a piece of paper; whether you send it through your body or your tongue.)

The best line from the Gitelman essay: "It has become common in popular usage to talk about the analog as the category that covers everything that isn't digital; but in fact most things are neither. *The images, sounds, smells, and so on that we live among have mostly not been reduced to information yet.*"

(Emphasis my own.)

Works Cited:

Gitelman, Lisa. Chapters 3–4. In *Always Already New: Media, History, and the Data of Culture*, 89–150. Cambridge, MA: The MIT Press, 2008.

Lavagnino, John. "Digital and Analog Texts." In *A Companion to Digital Literary Studies*, 402–414. Hoboken, New Jersey: Wiley-Blackwell, 2007.

THE MOST EXCITING MOMENT OF ALMA'S LIFE

New fiction from the short story giant.

By Etgar Keret

The most exciting moment of Alma's life occurred at the Jerusalem Biblical Zoo when she was less than seven years old. The Russian cage cleaner, later revealed to be an alcoholic, left a cage door open and its tenant used the opportunity to go out for a morning stroll.

And so Alma, who was waiting for her mother outside the zoo's whale-shaped restrooms, found herself standing less than ten meters from an African lion who answered to the name of Charlie. After a second of awkwardness, Alma smiled at the lion, who smiled back as he continued to move closer to her. Just when he was near enough for Alma to touch his mane, her mother, who had come out of the bathroom, gave a small cry and fainted.

The most exciting moment in Tsiki's life was when he proposed to Alma. His hands were all sweaty and the rhyming proposal he had prepared didn't come out as funny as he thought it would. When he was done, she gave him the small smile she always smiled when she was really stressed. Looking at her clenched lips, Tsiki was sure she was racking her brain for some non-insulting way to say "No." But what she finally said was "Why not," which is not as clear-cut as "Yes," though it was enough to make Tsiki's heart do a somersault in his chest.

There's something a little unfair in life. And I'm not talking about the botched abortion Alma had in high school that left her unable to have children. I'm talking about Alma and Tsiki's most exciting moments. It's a little unfair that their most exciting moments in life didn't overlap, not to mention that they happened so long ago that there's really nothing to look forward to. Sure, Alma can still fantasize about what her life would have been like if her mother hadn't appeared at that moment. And Tsiki must definitely have moments when he wonders what would have happened if Alma had refused his proposal. But those questions are just questions.

Though for Alma, it's not really just a question. Sometimes she actually dreams about what happened at the Biblical Zoo. She with her braids and the lion standing so close to her that she could feel his warm breath on her face. In some of the dreams, the lion rubs up against her in a friendly way, in others, he opens his mouth and roars, and then she usually wakes up terrified. So one can say that as long as she keeps dreaming, that moment hasn't completely passed. But dreaming, with all due respect, is not exactly living.

Translated by Sondra Silverston

14

BINARY PLANETS

A timeline of twinship, together and apart.
Writing by Ogechi Egonu and Ugochi Egonu,
illustrations by Elly Malone

As twins, we've been at each other's side for our whole lives. We know each other like the back of our hands, and with just a glance, we can tell exactly what the other is thinking. Our love has taken us through joys and tears—and given us space to grow into our own selves, too. This timeline celebrates the memories we've shared and how they've affected our relationship as sisters.

BIRTHDAY PARTY, AGE SIX

Soundtracked by Nigerian pop music, R&B, and Radio Disney, we danced the day away in our matching red blouses and freshly braided hair. We had invited practically the whole Bay Area Igbo community, and our mom still pulled random kids from the park to get a slice of our extra-large Costco cake. That day felt like the perfect combination of each of our worlds: school friends, church friends, and friends from the neighborhood.

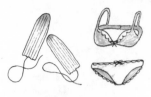

FIRST PERIOD

UGOCHI When I finally got my period, I was 12 years old. I had been anticipating it for a really long time and thought I was late to the period party. I remember waking up one morning, seeing the blood, and getting extremely excited. I thought having my period would somehow make me more sophisticated or adult-like, but after the first day I realized I was the same old Ugochi, just bloodier.

OGECHI The day I woke up to Ugochi getting her period, I was livid. Prior to that, Ugochi and I were weirdly excited for puberty and used to page through puberty books and talk breathlessly about *the journey of womanhood*. We would have long discussions about the best places to stash our theoretical pads/tampons and bonded over pseudo-scientific tips that claimed to grow boobs faster (which included chugging milk, scarfing down ramen with spinach, and fervent praying). Because I was older (by one minute!), I thought I'd get my period slightly before her—or I could agree to us getting it at *exactly* the same time. We did every single thing together, buying matching training bras and even losing our baby teeth, but Ugochi getting her period first was a physical reminder that we were growing—and it wouldn't always be at the same time.

That day I gave her the silent treatment and only broke it to comment on how she was definitely PMSing or to mutter that she was a traitor. I calmed down by the second day, because I realized she could now fill me in on what it was *really* like to have a period. When mine came a few months later, I was thoroughly underwhelmed but happy to have another thing in common with my sister once more.

THE START OF SEVENTH GRADE

Seventh grade was the first time our mom gave us free rein on what we could wear. We pored over teen-girl magazines to carefully create our *image*. Style became an important outlet for us to figure out who we were, and to experiment with the different personalities that came with different looks.

OGECHI I made it my goal to stand out. This translated into a signature outfit of bright patterned shirts, sequined flats, and a little bit of lipstick if our mom wasn't looking too closely (she still enforced a strict no-makeup rule). Meanwhile, Ugochi went for the unofficial middle-school uniform of skinny jeans and a fitted V-neck T-shirt. We were still each other's best friend but something felt a little different. Ugochi would casually mention one of her friends from the "cool crowd," and I would give an obligatory eyeroll. I couldn't believe she'd want to be friends with the same kids who thought my carefully crafted ensembles were something to ridicule. That was the first time I felt like people saw us as juxtaposing personalities: Ugochi as the "cool" sister and me as the "weird" one.

UGOCHI Seventh grade was one of the most cringeworthy times of my life, featuring the usual overly glossed lips and obsession with boy bands. It was the first (and last!) time that other people's opinions really mattered to me. I stopped wearing the purple fedora from the Walmart children's section that I adored, and instead chose Forever 21 skinny jeans that every other girl in my class wore. I tried my hardest to look and act like the girls who didn't care about me. I had nothing in common with them, but because they were the *popular girls*, I wanted their approval. Being with an unsupportive group of friends—people who didn't really know me—felt alienating. I was so grateful to have my sister and be around someone who cared more about me than what some boy in the hall thought.

BOARDING SCHOOL

For high school, we both decided to go to a boarding school on the other side of the Bay Area. Boarding school was kind of a rite of passage in our family: our mom went to one in Nigeria, and our brother went to one in Pennsylvania, so it felt right for us, too. We were both so ready to experience a change of pace and have our first taste of independence. The summer before we left was filled with *Zoey 101, All I Wanna Do,* and Harry Potter, aka "research for school."

Our meticulous preparation didn't do much—as it turns out, a magical castle with a Forbidden Forest is not a good stand-in for a school in a homogeneous and quaint town. Despite moving from a diverse city, we never really got homesick. Of course, we craved our mother's traditional Nigerian food and missed our friends back home, but we still had each other. Together, we made friends, crammed for tests, and complained about Italian Tuesday at the dining hall. It was a huge comfort to know the other was right there, ready to marvel at the number of white people in our classes or carry on long conversations analyzing the latest Childish Gambino album.

DISCOVERING WRITING

UGOCHI In sophomore year, I was having my teenage identity crisis: I was tired of being known as a twin and wanted to set myself apart from Ogechi. I got really interested in writing and participated in poetry slams and the spoken-word community. I loved it, and I started to define myself as The Writer.

The next year, Ogechi began competing in the same poetry slam, and I couldn't help but feel a little territorial. Writing and performing felt like a special part of *my* identity, and all of a sudden, the person I was trying to differentiate myself from was doing the same thing! I found myself getting bitter and jealous when she did well, instead of supporting her the way she did for me. But after watching her perform and seeing how hard she worked on her poems, I realized I was being unfair. Ogechi had just as much of a right as I did to explore creative outlets. Now, I am always the loudest person in the crowd, snapping and cheering whenever Ogechi is onstage. It took a while, but I finally figured out I didn't need to prove to anyone—myself most of all—that we were different from each other.

OGECHI I've always had a love for words: reading all kinds of books in the public library, journaling, doing plays and mono-logues. Since Ugochi had claimed writing as her thing, I felt like I wasn't allowed to like it, too. So I'd write poems in my head or in the margins of my math homework but never took it seriously. Oddly enough, what inspired me to share my writing publicly was Ugochi. Her poems were about owning who she was, and she always looked so in control performing. As I got more into spoken word, my fears of stepping on her toes were put to rest. With the thousands of words in the English dictionary, we have plenty of space to each develop separately as writers.

FAMILY EMERGENCY

Our brother, Michael, is undoubtedly the family favorite. With his outgoing attitude and acceptances to top-tier colleges, he's what our relatives want their kids to be, and someone we all look up to. When he was diagnosed with stage IV lymphoma in November 2015, it shook our whole family.

UGOCHI I kept telling myself that it wasn't real, the doctors had somehow misdiagnosed him. I tried to handle it the same way I handled other emotional situations: to move on and act as if nothing had happened. I knew Michael didn't want us to make a big deal out of it. So I tried to act normal and joke around with him, but everything felt forced.

When we went back to school, I broke. I tried to suppress my feelings, but I couldn't deny that I was terrified. I spent a good portion of that year crying alone and not knowing how to process my emotions. I finally realized that I needed to talk to someone.

OGECHI When we found out about Michael, we had just been confirmed into the Catholic Church. In confirmation class we learned about the seven sacraments, which is basically a bucket list of holy things to achieve before you die (confirmation is the second step). I remember being really confused: here was my brother, who had just started college and whom I saw as so full of life, now possibly staring at the end of it. This wasn't how the order of sacraments was supposed to go.

Our family turned to prayer: nightly rosaries around Michael's bed, my mom randomly dousing the house in holy water, anything to provide us with some sense of control. But what had once felt comforting now felt suffocating. I didn't have the same confidence in God that had prompted me to get confirmed. I felt hollow.

OGECHI AND UGOCHI As cliché as it sounds, even in dark times there is always light. In the hardest year in our lives, we were each other's light to see our way through. We healed *together*. Sometimes with teary-eyed talks about how tough it was to balance our fears for our brother, school, and our outside lives. Sometimes with movie marathons and candy. We grew closer to our family, Skyping often just to check in. We prayed, and slowly, the act felt meaningful again. In June, Michael went into remission.

SUMMER CAMP

The summer before senior year, we each pursued subjects we were passionate about, and we each traveled far away from home. That was the longest time we had ever spent apart, but we both agreed it was the best summer of our lives.

UGOCHI I went to a writing camp, where I made an amazingly talented group of friends, who were all so invested in their craft. We bonded over our love for beat poets and feminist writers. It was strange at first, because I was so used to feeling like the only person who understood my feelings was the person who lived through those experiences with me: my sister. It was refreshing to meet people who didn't see me as Ugochi-and-Ogechi, but just Ugochi. Nobody could compare me to her, or mix the two of us up. I was free to be Ugochi, to discover different parts of myself as a writer and an individual. The last day of camp was bittersweet.

OGECHI I left California for the first time to go to a Mandarin immersion program in Mississippi. Without Ugochi I was free to be just Ogechi, instead of Ogechiwhere'syoursister. Our time apart helped me find myself. I befriended people entirely different from me, discovering a world completely outside of my Bay Area bubble. That humid Southern summer was filled with all-nighters memorizing words until they jumbled together, dance parties to twerk away the stress, and a worrying amount of pizza. I wouldn't have wanted it any other way.

THE FUTURE

UGOCHI When we were in elementary school, Ogechi and I made a plan to be next-door neighbors and marry another set of twins. But after 17 years of being attached at the hip, we've abandoned that plan. We'll always be best buds, but applying to different colleges and continuing to grow on our own—like traveling to other parts of the world—is something I'm excited for.

OGECHI Although we had a pact to go to different colleges, we still ended up applying to a lot of the same ones. But even if we wind up at separate schools (and I hope we do), it doesn't mean we'll *feel* more distant. We've gone through it all and a few miles between us won't keep me from finding a way to borrow half the clothes in Ugochi's closet. With FaceTime and Skype and everything else, my sister won't ever be too far away.

BEYOND SELF-RESPECT

I had lost respect not for me, but for him.

By Jenny Zhang

My first boyfriend wore a stack of black rubber bands criss-crossed in an *X* formation on his wrists. "One for each time I was dumped," he told me and when I didn't show enough concern, he added, "Each one represents a different suicide attempt." He was dead serious and expected sympathy, which he got. I was 14 and hadn't questioned the validity of the idea that a girl not wanting to date a guy could potentially cause his *death*, but years later, it did occur to me that whenever someone broke my heart, whatever crushing feelings of sadness I experienced I'd blame on myself, not the person who rejected me. At first, I found his fragility hot, a welcome respite from the gross displays of masculinity the other boys in my school exhibited. He was the lead singer in a straight-edge hardcore screamo band whose songs were mostly about hot girls who didn't want to be with him. Once, when we walked past a group of black kids listening to rap on their boombox, he said, "You know why I don't like rap? Because it's *crap*."

"Wow," I should have said, "you're not funny *and* you're racist!" but instead I smiled and fake laughed as if it were the cleverest joke I'd ever heard. The things I thought we had in common (namely an affinity for weirdo punks and a distaste for the popular kids) were soon revealed as false. I started to suspect he got into the straightedge hardcore music scene to prey on girls and persuade them to date him and that he talked shit about the popular girls not because they were cruel to any kid who was poor, fat, and/or not white, but because they thought highly of themselves and didn't give him the time of day. After we broke up, a friend of mine told me she had gone to a show where his band was playing and he had dedicated his newest song to "that bitch who broke my heart." The next day when I saw him in the hallway, he had added a fresh black rubber X to his wrist. A part of me was hurt, a part of me was defensive, and another part of me just found him pathetic. Still, we got back together a year later and he was as bitter, pitiful, and whiny as he had been the year before. Was it because I didn't respect myself that I went back to him? Like many girls testing out the relationship waters, I was ambivalent. I liked him but I also found him to be beneath me. Even though the other kids at school didn't like me very much, and even though girls of color are not rewarded for exhibiting pride in themselves, deep down, buried under layers and layers of self-loathing and self-doubt, I believed in my own creativity, intelligence, and worth.

That same year, there was a mandatory schoolwide assembly to spread HIV awareness and prevention. One of the speakers told us she found out she was HIV positive after a man convinced her not to use a condom during sex. She had one major takeaway, directed at all the girls: "Don't expect a guy to respect you if you don't respect yourself!" I might have taken that advice to heart if not for the boys in my class who, before, during, and after the assembly, loudly and shamelessly referred to her as a "whore who loved getting it raw" and "a slut who was too ugly to have contracted AIDS" and worse. What did it matter for girls to respect ourselves when a boy was always lurking nearby to remind us that our worth was directly tied to how fuckable we were? What kind of self-respect is possible in a society that constantly bombards girls with the message that being too fuckable made you a slut and being too unfuckable made you a hag? Hearing those boys talk that way made me feel shame, but more than that, I wanted them to feel shame, too. I wanted to find a way to convey my disrespect for them, and I wanted it to sting.

In college, I regularly got into relationships with guys who made me feel both desired and demeaned. One boyfriend, after winning first place in a coveted writing contest that I had placed third in, told me, "Don't worry, one day you'll be as good as me." It was meant to be sweet, but I was insulted. "*One day?*" I raged to my friends. "I'm *already* better than him," and I meant it, too. I found him low-key misogynistic (whenever I pointed out anything was sexist, he'd tell me that I was behaving in a "scary manner") and racist (the one time he sat through a five-minute conversation between me and another Chinese American immigrant about shared foods we loved, he complained of feeling "totally left out and shunned," even though every single day, I sat through long conversations with him and his white friends as they referenced foods and cultural references I didn't know anything about), and found his writing high-key corny as hell. I didn't need him to reassure me that I would be as good as him one day; what I wanted was for him to acknowledge that he would be goddamn *lucky* to be as good as *me* one day.

Another (white) boyfriend claimed he never really considered whether or not his pattern of exclusively dating Asian women was problematic, and when I pushed him to explain why he was so attracted to Asian girls, he finally admitted, "Because they're just easier to handle." Despite losing respect for him after hearing that, I continued to date him for several months. Then there was a short-lived affair with a much older TA who was flirtatious, not just with me, but with all the female students who showed up to his classes in full makeup and their best outfits. After the initial thrills of secrecy and transgression wore off, I noticed how much he delighted in receiving attention from young women my age. For a man who was pushing 40, it wasn't a cute look. Years later, I'd run into him and without fail he was always with a fresh, new young woman, always between the ages of 19 and 23. I'm aware this makes me sound like the stupid girl who falls for her teacher and thinks she's *so* special, only to realize her teacher routinely and indiscriminately preys on girls, taking advantage of an unequal power balance where the scales tip in his favor. I probably was an insecure little girl looking for attention, but what about him? Wasn't he an insecure *grown* man looking for attention? Validation? Young flesh? Someone he could impress easily? Shouldn't a 40-year-old man be responsible for fixing that about himself before we ask it of a 19-year-old girl?

For teenage girls, the burden of respect is assumed to be theirs and theirs alone. They're told it's the number-one thing they must do for themselves if they want to be loved, but why do girls have to respect themselves before they are ever accorded any? Did teenage girls invent, on their own, impossible standards of beauty, intelligence, youth, innocence, responsibility, kindness, humility, and subservience? And for all the emphasis on respect, rarely are teenage girls called upon to elaborate *their* expectations and requirements for respect. Much of the time, celebrity couples who were once #RelationshipGoals, post-breakup, turn out to be mostly examples of men who have not earned the right to be loved by the women who love them. What would it even mean to earn the love and respect of a woman? These aren't questions we ask of girls or the society they are brought up in; instead, we distill the ills of patriarchy and misogyny down into a watery slogan of self-empowerment: *Respect yourself!*

"You're losing respect for him, and once you've lost the respect, it's hard to gain it back," my friend texted when I found myself falling in love with someone who was dealing with some pretty ancient pain that kept him from having a long-term relationship with ... well, pretty much anyone before he met me. He had commitment issues, fear of intimacy, repressed trauma, and a whole host of other problems that were threatening the stability of our relationship, and to put it bluntly, I was *done* with having energy-depleting relationships with men who couldn't deal with their own shit. "I'm thirty-fucking-three years old," I vented to my friends. "I don't have time for this. I can't be with someone who is afraid to know themselves. I don't have time to teach another guy how to be unrepressed. I don't have the energy to teach these emotionally stunted dudes who made it to adulthood without having to ever be accountable to anyone, including themselves." And it was true—I didn't. I was tired of being the person in relationships who had to own up to my issues and insecurities, which would then be weaponized against me, without any reciprocity.

So when my friend texted that perhaps I had lost respect not for *me*, but for *him*, I felt a sudden clarity. She said the thing no teacher, no authority figure, and certainly no man has ever advised me to consider: If someone wants to be with me, they have to earn my respect *and* honor my expectations and requirements for respect.

The way we talk about respect and teenage girls needs to change. I want girls to learn how to disrespect the men in their lives who cause them harm and violence, I want them to learn how to disrespect patriarchal values that bind and demean. Looking back on my past relationships, I can pinpoint the very moment when I lost respect for the person I was dating. Often, it happened early on—a casually offensive remark that betrayed deeper levels of racism, an unfunny joke that revealed how much he feared and hated women, or even just a delusional comment that showed zero self-awareness—but always, when I was younger, I would continue to date that person, doubling down on my commitment, all the while losing respect for him. That's the most disturbing part, that I thought I could love someone I didn't even respect.

After my conversation with my friend, I told the person I was seeing at the time that I needed to respect him again if this was going to work. "There are things you've done and said that have caused me to lose respect. And I can't love you if I don't respect you." It was true, I could not, and if that's the problem with girls these days, then . . . good for us.

FOR AMY
AND OTHER WOMEN
WHO CARRY CHAOS.

By Bassey Ikpi

If you are silent about your pain, they'll kill you and say you enjoyed it.
—Zora Neale Hurston

this flame and flicker
was not meant to last this long
we were not meant to chase the sun this often
uncertain, as we are, that the days will occur without us
so we wake
and lift
and push
and throw our bodies across these minutes
collecting respectable stacks of time
we wish to be praised for "trying"
maybe someone will call us brave
or strong
or marvel about how we are not like this one
or that one
sure that those whispers do not touch our skin

drugs.
booze.
men that hate you for loving them.

all this to dull the ache of living.
say we are worth this trouble that we cause
say you will love us until the chaos slides off our bones
lie if you must

we like the weight of water
appreciate how tidal waves mimic our moods
carry our hearts out to sea
seek life raft
seek buoy
return shipwrecked
splintered debris
saltwater and bloodstained
we try
every morning new beginnings
then crawl hands and knees back to our beds
when night falls
call out to god, jehovah, allah
pray someone will tell jesus, buddha, muhammad
anyone who answers when we are at war with ourselves.

choose drugs.
choose booze.
choose men who hate us for loving them
say we are worth this trouble we cause
say if we pray hard enough this chaos will slide off our bones
lie if you must

it is only a matter of time before we stop bleeding
they will ridicule the stains on our sheets
before the ache has fully left us
they will ask us what we did to cause this
why we couldn't welcome sun like the rest of the world

why we turn to men and drugs and booze
instead of god and work and money
nobody has the heart to tell them for us
we did not choose this.
did nothing to deserve or invite this beast in
we did not request our footprints on the sun
this chaos we wear on our heads
this life is neither punishment
nor reward
your life turns palm over fist
easy like judgment
we fight ourselves
avoid our palms
duck our fists
just so we can live the life you ease into
so that we can make it out alive
unbroken
scarred a little less

so just tell us
tell us that we're worth this trouble we cause
say that this chaos will one day slide off our bones
lie if you must

UNREQUITED

Celebrating the emo(tional) meme.
By Kiana Kimberly Flores

I regard writing as a secret act of confession. A way to make sense of the tangled-up parts of life. My disposition easily throws me into the abysmal habit of scribbling or typing words. Too often it has not been fun, contrary to what others imagine; contrary to what I myself would have believed. I tried devising ways of making writing more "fun," which turned out to be a total waste of time, but at least I was doing something.

I wrote notes-to-self letters, letters-from-my-past-self letters, letters-for-when-I'm-lonely letters as early as the age of nine. I had been secretly reading Jennifer Lynch's *The Secret Diary of Laura Palmer*, a romantic (to me) annotation of a mysterious girl's daily life, because I liked having secrets to and for myself. The book spearheaded my obsessive diary-writing phase, but I gradually went back to letter writing, as I found the typical diary format a bit too much for my developing mind. Letter writing did the job of laying out emotions that might have caused my voice to break, or feelings too extreme that brought my hands to shake, and translated them onto the page, seamless and stealthy. The only question was to send or not to send. Shakespeare was right-ish, after all.

The first time I wrote a letter addressed to someone else was on the first day of 2015. I was a college sophomore, cocooned neatly in the idea of romantic love: the kind that defies all rules and law, of man and of god; the kind that writers would write and clamor about, or balk at, if writers ever really do such things; the kind that poets would die for, if poets ever really die. The rationale was that I wanted to be loved like I deserved it.

I wrote the letter on papers torn hastily from my journal as I flitted back and forth from my dresser to my room, where all the books sleep with me, looking for the blackest black T-shirt that I own. I wrote forcefully, hellbent on ending the ordeal until it became a task—a heavy, leaden feeling sitting in my chest. I may or may not have cried.

I spent the first week of 2015 casually trying to redirect all my attention into not sending the letter. I obsessively ran errands, even when I had no actual errands to run. I thought that in writing, in letting him know what had happened to me, I would be granted some sort of freedom. On that paper, I'd scribbled a list of why I'd fallen for him and why I had proceeded to run away with that truth. There's always something about falling in love, even more so falling in love from afar, that keeps me agog—an unexpected hand hold, an eye contact so earnest you wanna spend a day with them before sunrise in Vienna, the same favorite book. Until feelings evaporate. Until certain glorious moments spent with someone become an exaggerated, over-edited manuscript to the story in my head. Chris Kraus in *I Love Dick* resonates: "Does analogy make emotion less sincere?"

I wish I could redeem myself by telling you I sent the letter. Too bad I'm not a great liar. The five-page missive remains unsent, tucked in my journal with the little green leafy curlicues on the cover. Each time I rummage through my notebooks, the letter haunts me; in the way that *The Shining* haunts me or everyone else I know: its gallons and gallons of Kensington Gore bursting forth; how the letter could open a floodgate of emotions right into the hotel lobby of my beating heart. I thought that transforming something intangible into a physical manifestation would propel him to fall in love with me—an end-all, be-all solution, or the only solution there was. More Kraus: "What seemed so daring just looks juvenile and pathetic." On that day, I felt small, crouched over my bed, scratching the paper with gusto, mind zipping all over the place.

What is nice to believe in theory isn't viable in practice. Like romantic love (the advertised neon-sign one, at least), or carrying a torch for someone who wasn't even there, or has no intentions of going there. Too often I've subscribed to these ideals, and the effect was always heartbreak. I thought I'd gained freedom in writing that junk mail—and I did. It wasn't a path for this guy and me to hold hands romantically while strolling on the beach, I've decided, but a reminder of myself on that first day of the year—how capable I felt. How geared I was to feeling what Terence McKenna, in his talk "Unfolding the Stone: Making and Unmaking History and Language," called "the shamanic dance in the waterfall."

I wanted to be loved like I deserved it, but the route I took was one in bad faith—a superficial love wrapped in a shiny box with a golden ribbon tied around it. If I wanted to be loved like I deserved it, I wouldn't have gone through highways of trouble for another person; my basic existence would've sufficed. (Or, will it?) I wonder if this is the love chronicled in that 1 Corinthians verse ("Love is patient, love is kind . . .")? But then, I've figured that if I can traverse hell or swim high waters *for someone,* surely I could do the same for myself one day. I trust and hold this feeling like a talisman.

I have this fear that writing down my feelings—especially Serious Romantic Feelings—and sending them to my subject of affection would make me come off as a meme. A rather emo(tional) one. That pouring out my feelings would make them sticky like maple syrup: clichéd. Like staring at a sunset for far too long until the afterglow demanded an exegesis. *Does analogy make emotion less sincere?* This aversion to Feelings boggled my day-to-day existence when it wasn't even worth being boggled about, so I've since accepted that I am a meme of my own—and resolve to be forevermore—and yes, I am emo(tional) as heck. The world tells me ridiculous things about being too lonely, too feel-y, too grandiose, even. A tired tale of being too much, where writing diaries is "vying for attention" and laughing loudly in public is "so un-ladylike." But going on tangents for and about my feelings is my way of furthering who I am, whoever I may be at any given moment: obsessed teen girl, prolific letter writer, woman, person.

My letter to a boy debunked what I thought were steel-sure beliefs on romantic love. I grew up enchanted by it, believing it was the rule. One can hold on to a belief so much—until one falls in love, writes a letter, and refuses, or is daunted, to send it. I didn't get to let a boy know that I hurt and ached and mourned. He didn't get to write back, or not. He did not get to say, "Fuck you, crazy girl, what is wrong with you." People told me I wasn't in a position to cry over or have my heart broken by unrequited love because (a) "Honey, it wasn't his fault that you loved him," (b) "Girl, he did not ask to be loved," and (c) "Oh man, just get it over with! It was unrequited anyway." Does reciprocity make emotion more sincere?

YOU FIRST

On cultivating emotional fortitude.
By Danielle Henderson

There's a feeling that you have learned to ignore. It's the one that starts as a dull throb in the deepest part of your body, stretching symphonic tendrils of "NO" toward your heart, often subsiding into a disappointing chorus of "who cares" by the time it gets there. The feeling hits hardest when you're trying to put yourself first—you don't want to go to the movies tonight, but you're afraid to hurt your friend's feelings if you say no. You always seem to do what your partner wants to do on a Friday night, but isn't that the way you show love?

Several times a day, in the span of approximately 10 seconds— from the first electric rumblings to the spectacular fizzle—you accomplish something that took our ancestors centuries to develop. You push forward and ignore your instinct to love yourself first.

Most people will confidently tell you to love yourself without giving you any firm directions on how to *actually* do it. The concept of self-love has been whittled down to self-care, and self-care has been reduced to a buzzword—it's an opportunity to sell face masks and fancy moisturizers more than it is an invitation to develop any sort of emotional intelligence. Nothing is wrong with a pedicure, but a smooth foot means fuck all if you haven't learned how to love yourself from within.

Learning how to say no means you have to learn how to set boundaries; it's probably the most important part of self-care, and something most people never quite manage to learn. Part of the problem is that setting boundaries sounds harsh—like you're throwing up a brick wall between yourself and the world—but the dictionary definition of emotional intelligence is all about your capacity to control and express your emotions. The boundary-making part of your emotional intelligence is really a matter of figuring out what you want before you actively engage with someone else's idea of a good time.

I really learned how to say no as an act of boundary-setting self-care in high school. The teenage life can be a highly regulated one, thanks to parents, teachers, and after-school jobs; since I only had about five hours to myself each week, I grew to be fiercely protective of my free time. No, I absolutely did not want to go to a football game—I wanted to sit at home and watch some *The Kids in the Hall* episodes I'd taped that were bound to be way more entertaining than watching the guys who threatened me all week throw themselves around a field. Why would I want to go to a party and stand around awkwardly while everyone else drank themselves into a stupor when I could drag my sewing machine to the kitchen table and try out that new French seam I read about at the library? Admittedly, I only knew that these things were not fun for me because I had tried them in the past; developing a strong sense of self involves taking risks or trying new things. But it's totally OK if you hate those things once you've tried them.

I felt like a bit of a weirdo for not finding joy in the typical teenage things I was supposed to love, but I kept the FOMO at bay by doing things that were guaranteed to make me happy. It feels strange trusting yourself at an age when most people are still telling you what to do, but that's even more of a reason to lean into boundary-setting self-care as a personal ritual—you're setting a template that will last the rest of your life.

Loving yourself first is not always about saying no; emotional boundaries are often more about saying *yes* to what you want. It was easy for me to forgo football games, because spending four hours practicing how to sew made me feel good for *days*. I wanted to be a good seamstress so that I could make all of the outfits that were floating around in my brain, so it made sense to me to spend as much time as possible learning that craft. I didn't know it then, but I was saying *yes* to something that would sustain me for the rest of my life—the ability to translate the ideas in my head into items that exist in the real world. Considering it's literally how I make a living now, I think it was a good choice.

When you get in the habit of setting boundaries and loving yourself first, it profoundly affects the direction of your life simply by forcing you to pay more attention to how things make you feel. You start to notice friendships that are one-sided, or learn how to roll your heart-eyes at people who threaten to steal your shine. Emotional vampires take a backseat to the people in your life who elevate you. When I was 18, I figured out that some of the people who were dragging me down the hardest were members of my own family. Things had always been fraught between my mother and me since she left me at my grandparents' house when I was 10 and never came back, but I had never really considered writing her out of my life until I graduated high school. Nothing about our cultural conditioning can prepare you for a life without a mother (either by choice or by force), so it was a strange decision to make, but then I realized: *Trying to have a relationship with my mother makes me feel bad, so I'm not going to do it anymore.* I gave myself permission to change my mind, and even kept the door open to her for a long time, but in the end, I didn't need the limited kind of love she offered. I learned how to love myself enough for both of us.

The kind of emotional fortitude I get from loving and protecting myself also gives me a sense of confidence about how I move through the world. I trust that I'm always making the best decision about what I need, which takes the edge off of things like quitting jobs or deciding to put off college for more than a decade. This isn't to say that life is always easy—I really struggled for a long time before I was able to cobble together anything even resemblinga career. But leaving my shitty, volatile coffee-shop job to be an office assistant was a decidedly good thing, and leaving *that* office-assistant job to work for the United Nations was an even better decision. Every time I left a job, it was for one that would bring me closer to my goals, by either paying me more or being a better environment with better people in it. Stability, community, and happiness sometimes matter more than your paycheck.

Your boundaries will shift like the tide as you move through the world, but your gut feeling will rarely steer you in the wrong direction. You're going to live with yourself for the rest of your life, so love yourself fiercely.

MEMORY IS AN ANGEL
WHO CAN FLY NO MORE

Revelations, after the fact.
By Jackie Wang

It is strange what happens when you let go of the negative things in your life—something beautiful might enter.

Sometimes life hands you these ruptures, like a gift.

Like when B was fired from her job and within a week was offered a new job that paid more, required her to work less, and was more enjoyable.

"I didn't realize how unhappy I was until they fired me."

It was like that with my last relationship, too.

I didn't realize how unsatisfying it was until it was over.

But now that I am focusing on the things I love and surrounding myself with people who make me happy, I can't help but dwell on the question: *Under what conditions do I betray myself so deeply?*

I was slow to love you. It came over me in fits and starts. It was not automatic, like my other loves, but a seedling that grew out of little moments of togetherness: sitting next to you as you sat with perfect posture practicing Bach on the piano, reading Pier Paolo Pasolini poems to each other in bed, shopping for the perfect toy gift for your little sister. I can pinpoint the moment I first felt love for you, but now I feel nothing. The reality of you is fading. I remember that there was love, but this love is like a newspaper clip buried in the garden; the words and image barely legible. It is right to let you go, and yet when I think back to that inaugural moment I wonder if you actually loved me then, or how it is possible that an experience that felt so true when it was lived could be corrupted by what came later.

A memory is not the fact of what occurred. Memories live in an ecosystem and are transformed by events that interact with our memories. The whole of the relationship is the context in which the memory lives.

TAKE ONE

One night, toward the beginning of my relationship with M, we were in my bed discussing the complexity of sibling love. I started to talk about the films of Bertolucci, how I loved a particular scene in *Me and You* where Olivia—the fucked-up, junkie older half sister of the adolescent misanthrope Lorenzo—grabs her brother and holds his face while singing David Bowie's "Ragazzo Solo, Ragazza Sola" (the Italian version of "Space Oddity").

He was touched by the video. We played the Bowie track over and over, looked up the Italian lyrics and playfully sang along, tumbled around in bed exaggeratedly rolling our *R*s. We said Italian was the most beautiful language in the world.

This is how a shared fragment of media became an entry in the book of our love.

But memories are not stable. A memory can be warped, maimed, and mangled; it can undergo a transformation.

What do revelations do to what has already occurred?

There are betrayals small and large, bruises of varying magnitudes—but it's the smaller one I return to today because of how completely it upended my sense of reality—what I thought to be true.

What I believed to be true, what you told me.

You said you had a friend.

You said you slept with this friend's girlfriend.

I asked you how you could remain friends after sleeping with his girlfriend.

You said, *He doesn't know.*

Later you said, *Never mind. I lied. I never slept with his girlfriend.* You said you needed this lie.

You said you had stopped talking to the woman half a year ago. You said she continued to write and flirt with you, but you didn't respond.

You lied about that, too.

This revelation was not what disappointed me most.

How do I become emotionally invested in the falsehoods and
   illusions people feed me even when I can see through
   them?
I needed to believe that the one I loved was separate from the
   one who wounded me
that I was a bystander who was caught in the crossfire of his
   self-hatred
Because I saw that he was suffering, I could not abandon him
   and after every spate of put-downs he would weep and
   apologize
Sometimes only my tears could break through his anger
   and then afterward he would collapse in guilt and cry out
   to me, "You don't even like me!"

And that call—I could not ignore it
   that primal call for love

I would accept the duty I was called to perform in those
   moments
As wounded as I was by his attacks I would comfort him

but after every episode a part of me would withdraw
from the relationship
My body would register these emotional betrayals
and over time it became harder and harder to feel
comfortable sharing myself with him
As I became more emotionally distant, his attacks became
more frequent and severe
Even when I knew that I could not trust him to handle my
heart with care
I stayed because I felt that his aggression was coming from a
place of feeling fundamentally unlovable
I stayed even when I realized that my existence as an
autonomous human being with her own needs and
feelings would drive him mad
I stayed until I had no energy left to prove to him that I still
loved him, the love had been crushed out of me
Do I believe, on some level, that I am stronger than I am,
that I won't be affected by hurtful behavior?
Maybe I believe that I can master every situation with my
perspicacious mind, acute power of observation, and
ability to analyze situations
Sometimes I use my intellect as a defense against the terror of
actually connecting to my feelings
Who is the Jackie I show to the world: *laid back, tolerant,
strong, rational*
What is beneath the facade:
loneliness as an ontological condition,
the deep sorrow of having been scorned and demonized
by my mother as a child
Do I love only the ones who leave me to my solitude?
The ones who don't notice when I am sad
or elsewhere in my head?
The ones who take the "me" I show them at face value

while privately I only feel understood in books?

Does anyone see me?

What is this intense longing for a witness that comes with a
vehement rejection of any such witness?

Since I was a child I have known that without the mirror of
the loving maternal gaze, I would have to witness myself

I would find a way to *make myself* in words.

TAKE TWO

Our romantic relationships are usually as dysfunctional and
chaotic as our childhoods.

That's why it's hardly surprising that people who have trust
issues are drawn to people who confirm their unconscious belief
that people are not trustworthy.

You asked me to trust you.

I said that it troubled me that you could lie without flinching.

To clear your name you showed me the messages you
exchanged.

When I pointed out more of your falsehoods, that you
were flirting during the period you claimed you were not
communicating at all

You said it was not a question of love, but a question
of domination that you were leading her on as revenge for
rejecting you.

But it was not the flirting games that wounded me most;

It was a video you sent her of the Bertolucci clip I showed you.

I asked you why you sent the video. *Don't you think it's
romantically suggestive?*

"Yes, but—"

The beautiful memory was ruined.

How does it feel

when you share something beautiful with someone

and it becomes part of the archive of your love?

People are not fungible.

The text that is generated between two people is singular.

The one who loves you shared something with you
> and this opening of the heart is an invitation to commune—
> a portal for you to step through.

Because Italian is the most beautiful language in the world,
> because sibling love is so complicated and weirdly tender,
> because we are new lovers—I show you the Bertolucci clip

and we roll around in bed singing the Italian lyrics of the Bowie
> song

But you take that very personal and meaningful thing I have
> shared with you

and cheapen it by using it as something you can leverage in a
> game of interpersonal war.

It is not just that you've tarnished the memory—
> the first time that I felt I loved you—

but it shows your preference for (or perhaps addiction to) a form
> of relatedness that is false.

James Baldwin says, "I can't believe what you say, because I see
> what you do."[1]

But it seems I must live by the dictum: *I believe what you say,
despite what you do.*

It is in this way that I, too, often find myself living a life that is
> false

because the fantasies enable me to gloss over the contradictions
> of my life and my decisions.

But now when I sift through what was once the archive of our
> love

All that remains is a heap of detritus

And a memory that no longer has wings.

1 From *The Devil Finds Work* (Vintage, 2011)

♥ BOOK LOVE ♥

Transport yourself.
By Emma Straub

When people fall in love, they disappear. We've all seen it—the friend who might as well have moved to Timbuktu because she can't do anything but gaze at her new beloved. Those friends emerge months or years later, blinking into the sunlight like lost moles, their new love softened by time into something that can beintegrated into the rest of their lives. This happens with platonic relationships, too—when you meet someone you're so obsessed with, so excited by, that you'd wear their skin if you could. For others, that self-erasing, vanishing kind of love is found most often in albums, or in television shows, or in the quiet dark of a movie theater. For me, though, it's not a scorching love affair, or a new BFF, or any of those things. For my money, nothing is more transporting—more *wait wait wait I don't want to leave just yet, one more minute please*—than a novel. There's something about the unadorned words on a piece of paper that let me slip inside other voices and lives—a magic trick hidden inside a modest rectangular object.

It's always been this way—I barely remember my childhood family vacations because I spent them all with my nose buried in Lois Duncan and Christopher Pike books. In high school, I read e. e. cummings until I could hardly recognize a capital letter. When I was in college, I went Russian for

months, and read only Tolstoy. There was my Jane Austen phase, and my Henry James phase, and my Edith Wharton phase. In grad school, I dove headfirst into Lorrie Moore. I brought six books on my honeymoon, including two Sookie Stackhouse mysteries, which were terrible. I read them anyway.

Of course, for writers, books are also road maps. If I tell you where I've been, where I'm going becomes clearer. The Christopher Pike and Lois Duncan books made me love plot and forward motion, and also ruined me for what I saw as their Disney-fied, scrubbed-clean competitor, R. L. Stine, whose stories always ended the way my stories for my three-year-old do, with a case of mistaken identity and no real harm done. e. e. cummings showed me that it was OK to let myself go wild, to ignore the rules, to play. Tolstoy showed me the pleasure of pain, and how satisfying loss can be. The Brits taught me about detached humor, about subtext, about letting the internal life bloom on the page. Lorrie Moore made me funnier, because I let myself tell the truth. I'm not sure what the Sookie Stackhouse books tell you about me—that I'm not a snob, I suppose, and also that I find Alexander Skarsgård's naked body extremely appealing. They're all as much a part of me as my small ears or loud, honking laugh or the beauty marks on my face that my sons poke with their tiny fingers.

Now that I have two small children and a life that doesn't offer endless (or even many) hours of uninterrupted reading, books are even more precious to me. I don't mean the parenting books, which I slog through, bleary-eyed at 10 PM, because I need to know how to make my child go back to sleep, or the books that I'm asked to read for blurbs. Each book that I choose to read for pleasure has to grab me so fiercely that it's impossible for me to put down—if at earlier points in my life, I read for energy (see: Allen Ginsberg), or beauty (see: Jhumpa Lahiri), or some dramatic love affair that I did not possess (see: *Madame Bovary*), right now I read for that most primal feeling: transportation, swift and overwhelming. The best part about being a writer/woman/parent/human is that there's no point at which the tank is full—if I'm going to go forward, to grow and learn as I go along, then I have to keep putting more gas in. I need to live inside other people's words and ideas, to see what their characters see, to fall from one line to the next in beautiful, endless adultery. I need to fall in love over and over again to remain committed to my job, as it were.

Right now, I'm in the midst of what I'm thinking of as a giant pet project, because it's less scary that way, if I think about it like a lark and not like an enormous life change with huge challenges at every step: I'm opening a bookstore. My local bookstore closed, and so my husband and I decided to open a new one. On paper (always on paper!), it seems simple. Get a room, or rooms. Fill those rooms with shelves and tables. Fill those shelves and tables with books. Open the door, and then watch people come in, pick a book, and get lost. The hard part is going to be choosing every book on those shelves, one by one, and placing them there, thousands of love affairs waiting to happen, thousands of tickets to Timbuktu, to another life, to transcendence, all of them waiting. Which one is waiting for you?

Emma's Top Five Right-This-Second Books You Should Read:
1. *A Visit from the Goon Squad*, Jennifer Egan
2. *The Colossus of New York*, Colson Whitehead
3. *Savage Beauty: The Life of Edna St. Vincent Millay*, Nancy Milford
4. *The Sisters: The Saga of the Mitford Family*, Mary S. Lovell
5. *The Secret History*, Donna Tartt

SUPER INTO A PERSON'S PERSON-NESS

A conversation between YA powerhouses on
writing epic—yet real—teen love.
By John Green and Rainbow Rowell

RAINBOW ROWELL You and I both write about teenagers in love—in big love—and that wasn't necessarily my story. Were you in love when you were 16?

JOHN GREEN I fell in love for the first time when I was 19, so when I write about romantic love among high school students, it is almost purely conjecture. Were you in big love? Didn't you start dating Kai when you were, like, 18?

RAINBOW No, I met Kai—now my husband—when I was 12. (TWELVE.) But we didn't start dating until after college.

JOHN I met my wife, Sarah, when I was 16, but we didn't even know each other in high school. She remembered me only as "the boy who smoked."

RAINBOW I didn't know you went to high school together! I think that I had fallen in love when I was 16, but not with one person and in one continuous way. I'm not sure how to explain that...

JOHN That is exactly how I feel, actually! I had fallen in love, but not in one continuous way. Yes. That's it.

RAINBOW I feel like I had really deep feelings that I didn't know how to process or organize. And big moments with people that I couldn't even recognize.

61

JOHN I definitely look back to some of the big moments in my high school life when I'm writing.

RAINBOW Yes.

JOHN But they weren't all focused on romantic love. There was this deep love I felt a few times, in little moments, and it felt better and more important than anything else in high school. And some of them involved sex or romance, but some of them didn't.

RAINBOW I had an idea of romantic love in high school that was so narrow—I didn't recognize it in my own life. Like, I thought people had to look and act a certain way.

JOHN Right. I believed that part of loving a girl was idealizing her, and romanticizing her, and treating her like a princess and whatever.

RAINBOW Yes—and, as a girl, being idealized!

JOHN I thought this was, like, my responsibility as a boy, to put the girls in my life on pedestals. But of course that is terribly destructive and dehumanizing.

RAINBOW I saw that so often in my male friends. I also felt like the boys in my life, especially, were casting their great loves. Like seeking out girls who fit their idea of who they should love. Girls do this, too.

JOHN For sure, but there's something about when boys do it that interacts with the larger structures of the social order in really disturbing ways.

RAINBOW I think my self-image was so bad that I actually couldn't see it when people liked me. Like, I couldn't even cast myself in that role.

JOHN The part that I find weird looking back is when we would all try to reshape each other to fit into the definition of a romantic partner, when the problem was with the definition.

RAINBOW This is a place where fiction got in my way. Mostly, fiction has saved my life. But it really gave me narrow ideas about romantic love.

JOHN Yes, me too.

RAINBOW Do you remember—did you do this?—talking or thinking about your TYPE?

JOHN Yes.

RAINBOW Like, your IDEAL?

JOHN Yes. I had a type. Everyone had a type.

RAINBOW I remember my friends and I trying so hard to DEFINE what we loved and were attracted to. BUT NONE OF US HAD ANY EXPERIENCE.

JOHN Which member of the Spice Girls was the one for me?

RAINBOW I remember saying ridiculous things, like, "For me, it's all about the hands—a guy has to have nice hands." ?????

JOHN Right. For me, it was noses.

RAINBOW Are you kidding?

JOHN Like, what in the actual fuck does that even mean? I wish I were kidding.

RAINBOW HAHAHAH.

JOHN I was big on a really top-quality human female nose.

RAINBOW I'm actually laughing out loud.

JOHN But the weirdest thing is that I had no built-in Platonic Ideal of the Nose or whatever. I was basing this definition of nasal beauty entirely on external forces.

RAINBOW Wow, you were so deep. And fresh. Like, anybody could say "legs."

JOHN I feel like I am being made fun of right now.

RAINBOW I thought I was making fun of you WITH you.

JOHN You are; it's fine.

RAINBOW So, OK, I actually have a thought about how this connects to writing.

JOHN OK.

RAINBOW When I'm writing love stories (which I can't help but do, it's always a love story for me), I really don't want to be writing a story that makes it worse for the people reading it. That perpetuates all the lies about love and attraction.

JOHN Right.

RAINBOW But also, if I'm writing about teenagers, I don't want them to be somehow magically above this bullshit. They can't be wizened 40-year-olds who know from experience that it's garbage.

JOHN Well, but also, I don't think you ever get magically above this bullshit. We're talking like this is all in our past, but of course inherited ideas about beauty and attractiveness affect adult life, too.

RAINBOW Yes.

JOHN Hopefully over time you develop an awareness that, e.g., your obsession with the perfect nose is completely ludicrous, but it's not like it all goes away.

RAINBOW You're still a nose man?

JOHN God, no. I am a PERSON MAN. I am super into a person's person-ness.

RAINBOW Excellent.

JOHN I hope, anyway. But you're right. The challenge is to write about adolescent experience in a way that's honest and not condescending, without underscoring the destructive parts of the romantic social order.

RAINBOW Thank you for saying that so eloquently.

JOHN But doing that is challenging. Like, I think I kind of failed at doing it in my first novel, *Looking for Alaska*. Like, I wanted that book to be about this boy's failure to understand the girl he liked complexly, and the catastrophic consequences of that failure.

RAINBOW "I think I kind of failed at that in my first novel—perhaps you've heard of it; it changed lives and inspired tattoos—*LOOKING FOR ALASKA*."

JOHN But I'm not sure it worked.

RAINBOW Go on.

JOHN Pudge idealizes Alaska the whole first half of that book, and in the second half, when he's grappling with the consequences, she's not around, so his understanding of her can only change so much. That's a lot of what I was thinking about when I started writing *Paper Towns*, which I tried to make expressly about the destructive consequences of failing to imagine other people complexly.

RAINBOW I'm not sure that you failed. Maybe you just didn't accomplish the entirety of what you were hoping to say.

JOHN Yeah, maybe. Writers are terrible at analyzing their own books, in my experience.

RAINBOW And maybe it's too much for Pudge to learn? Like, it would have been a real stretch for him to get to that sort of understanding? I think you read the book and get that he failed to see her and know her, as she was.

JOHN Thanks. I hope so!

RAINBOW I also think that we—or any writer—usually need more than one book to complete a thought.

JOHN One of the things you're really good at and that I really admire in your books is that you're able to create extremely realistic characters whose love feels real, but, at the same time, I as the reader understand the ways in which the characters' experiences are limited. It's not accurate exactly to say that your narrators are "unreliable" or whatever, but as a reader you see some of what the characters don't know, or can't look directly at. This is one of the hallmarks of great YA fiction to me, going back to *The Catcher in the Rye* and *The Outsiders*.

RAINBOW Geez, thank you. I think that's what we were talking about before—especially with teen characters—the attempt to write realistic characters who experience love and life authentically without projecting our adult perspectives onto them.

JOHN Right, but also giving them an arc, which *is* realistic. People do grow. That's the best part of my teen experience to me. I was talking earlier about those moments of deep love I experienced in high school and how formational they were for me . . . and I learned from them. I am still learning from them.

KARMA

The screen star and author on learning to love without shame.
By Gabourey Sidibe

So I really believe in karma. Like a lot. Possibly more than the average person. I believe if you do something bad, the universe will respond with quick and painful judgment to let you know that you fucked up. If you do something nice, you get nothing. Why should you be rewarded for being a decent human being, you scumbag? Just be happy you're alive. Or that you get to be happy, or something. I don't know. I try not to think about good karma too much. I just concentrate on the bad karma, because I really need it to stop messing with me. That might seem confusing to you because you know I'm super dope, but I assure you. There are some dark forces surrounding me and keeping me single.

Everything else is great! I have amazing friends, who I also consider to be my amazing family. I have a super-fun career that I'm excited about, and I have a million other things in my life that bring me happiness and wealth in ways that have nothing to do with money. But when it comes to my love life, I'm basically a boarded-up town that had to close the local factory. Everyone's out of work and soon they'll have to sell off a few children for scraps of bread. There's nothing here. I have no love life. None! My karma is keeping me out of a relationship, and I just have to live with that. All because of some shady stuff I did at 21.

Look. I get bored. A lot! I'm kind of always in the market for something to do and somewhere to be. This is not a big problem to have at my current age, 34, but it was a dramatic and troublesome weight on my shoulders when I was in my early 20s. I couldn't stand being bored. I couldn't stand to not have something my friends had. I couldn't stand not having someone to look at me. I was deep in my "ho phase," and I was sure that if I didn't have a "gentleman caller" like all of my friends (that's what we called them, because we were so fancy!), to look at me and want to have sex with me, I would just disappear. I would vanish into thin air as if I never existed because, at the time, I was dumb enough to think that I was nothing—unless some man could verify my existence. Any man. Whether or not I even *liked* that man had nothing to do with it.

The Ho Phase is so real and so taxing. I wouldn't recommend it but I wouldn't *not* recommend it, either. I learned some things.

So while I was out and about in my ho phase and also looking for any entertainment I could find, I auditioned for a college theaterproduction of *The Wiz*, at my friend Crystal's school, Lehman College, in the Bronx. I got the role of Glinda the Good Witch, which was great! Play rehearsal would keep me creatively entertained for three months, at least. And I really needed that. I had failed out of my own college while dealing with an almost crippling depression, and was now in an intensive six-month therapy program to help stuff my brain back in my ear and get my life on track. Outside of therapy Monday through Friday, from 11 AM to 4 PM, I was free to focus on making myself as happy as possible. I was learning that depression was my responsibility to overcome.

So I joined the play! The only bad thing was that I had to get to the Bronx every day for rehearsal and back home to Harlem, sometimes pretty late at night. Anyone who has ever tried to catch the train from one NYC borough to the next after 10 PM knows the struggle can get real. One night, after the long walk from the Lovinger Theatre, out of the college, across a bridge over abandoned trains on abandoned tracks, I crossed Bedford Avenue to get to the underground path to the opening of the Bedford train station, when a car pulled up to me. A voice called out, "Ay, girl! Can I drive you home?"

"For free?" I asked.

"Of course. I want to get to know you."

Listen. I definitely wouldn't recommend it, but I was 21, lazy, bored, and obviously not great at making decisions, so I definitely got in the passenger side of this stranger's car with very little questioning. Don't be like me with my "anything for a ride home"–ass attitude, readers.

So obviously I got in the car and we exchanged names. Against my better judgment, I told him my real name. I don't remember his, so let's call him . . . Robert. Robert asked if I was older than 18. Not "How old are you?" Nope. He wanted to know if I was of legal age. I knew immediately what Robert was about. I was 21 but looked about 16. Truancy officers still frequently stopped me during the day. Robert looked to be around 40, and that's saying a lot for a black dude. Turns out he was the same age as my mother. He asked if I minded his age. I didn't. I was thinking that no matter what this dude wanted from me, I was just getting this one ride home and then I would forget about him and move on. That's not what happened, though. (He didn't assault and murder me. That's not what happened, either. Thank god!)

Robert owned a car-service company and was driving me home in one of his vehicles. I wasn't impressed. He stated that he was a "good Christian man." *Hmmm. Sure you are, buddy.* He was divorced, with a 12-year-old daughter. I remember her age, because it was weird that he was picking me up when I was less than 10 years older than his daughter, whom he had sole custody of. Is that what *all* good Christian men do? I still wasn't impressed. He lived and worked in the Bronx, but he was interested in getting to know me, so if I ever needed a ride anywhere, all I had to do was call or text him. If I were ever going to be impressed by him, that would've been the statement to win me over. It didn't, but that was as good as it was going to get. My attention peaked at a free ride home. When he got to my building, I made him go around to the back, so that he couldn't identify it if he saw it in the daytime. I really thought I was thinking! We exchanged numbers, and as I got out of his car, I shook his hand and thanked him for the ride and purposely called him the wrong name. I truly thought I was done with him forever. But then I wasn't. I get *so bored*, y'all! Bad karma, here I come!

Robert turned out to be a deacon at his church. He was very preachy and would accuse me of being a bad Christian because I believed in scientific facts, like how the Earth revolves around the sun. He was filled with lectures on how to be a better Christian and a better woman, and how I needed to learn to be a mom to his 12-year-old. He'd drag me to church on Saturday (that's how some people do it!), and he'd take me to Bible study after rehearsals on weeknights, but when we were alone, he'd try his best to pressure me into having sex.

I told him I was a virgin, though. I *super* wasn't a virgin. I was just a liar. I didn't want to have sex with him. I really just liked him spending money on me, taking me to dinners and movies, picking me up from therapy (I told him I was a candy striper at the hospital—hooray, LIES!), driving me to play rehearsal, and taking me home afterward. That's all I wanted from him. Putting up with biblical lectures was enough. I wasn't going to have sex with him, too. I told him that I was waiting for marriage like a good Christian woman. He seemed to respect that, because he couldn't argue against it. Certainly not with his own "good Christian" act. Besides. I couldn't start having sex with him. I was busy doing it with this guy in *The Wiz*.

Theater people are so fun! They're artistic, imaginative, and frequently horny. So there was a guy who was part of the chorus.

He was already pretty cocky—let's call him Darryl. I thought I was grown alllll over Darryl during rehearsal breaks. I thought I was grown with Darryl in the stall of the farthest bathroom. I thought I was grown with Darryl in an abandoned classroom. I even thought I was grown with Darryl in the locked and dark adjoining theater.

I actually met Darryl and started acting grown with him before I met Robert. Why didn't I just keep walking when Robert so romantically called to me from his car? Because Darryl didn't want to publicly hold my hand or admit that anything was going on between us. He wanted to pretend to be grown with me for, like, 15 minutes (really like seven minutes), and then he wanted to go publicly flirt with the skinny Latinas in the play. So I got in Robert's car. Robert would take me on dates. He would introduce me as his girlfriend to his friends and family. I was terribly embarrassed, because I didn't want to be his girlfriend, and he knew that. I told him I *wasn't* his girlfriend, but he was public in a way with me that Darryl didn't want to be so . . . I guess I was taking what I thought I could get with Robert. But whenever I had 10 minutes (three minutes!) to spare at rehearsal, I settled for less than I wanted from Darryl.

I know that some of my behavior can be thought of as that of a young girl who doesn't quite understand relationships and doesn't yet know her self-worth, so maybe she should get a break before being dumped a truckload of bad karma. I want to think that, too, but I know the truth. This girl was a real piece of work.

So Robert was trying everything to sleep with me. He once asked if I'd ever thought about sex. I said, "Duh. But I'm still waiting until marriage."

He answered, "The Bible says that if you even *think* a sin, you've committed it in your heart." (The LOGIC!)

"You're saying that since I've thought about sex, I might as well just have sex with you, because I've already sinned in my mind and heart?"

"Exactly." He was dead serious.

I wasn't convinced and continued my farce of abstinence. Although . . . look. I *refused* to have sex with him, but I wasn't a nun, either. (Nothing serious. Mostly making out. I truly was and still am a late bloomer.) Where it really got tough was when he began to tell me he loved me. I'm not sure I as an adult believe he really loved me, but I believed it then. I believed he loved me. He seemed to show it, with gifts and fistfuls of cash. He did literally everything I ever asked of him. But I was nowhere near loving him. That's something I could've kept to myself, but I didn't. Every time he said, "I love you," I'd respond with a disgusted noise and say, "Don't bother." I was horrible. I was mean to him. When he introduced me as his girlfriend, I'd make that same noise and say, "The hell I am! Stop telling people that!" I openly flirted with younger friends of his who were closer to my age. I'd make him take my friends and me to dinner and pay for everything. He'd give me a gift, and I'd make fun of it in front of him. I'd hang out with my friends until 2 AM and call him to get out of bed and come get me. I was an asshole. I treated him the way I felt every time some cute but mean crush of mine, like Darryl, rejected me. I felt powerful treating him as if he were disposable. Like I was somehow exacting my revenge on everyone who didn't love me.

I don't want to absolve this dude of any skeeviness, by the way. He was nearly 50 years old and trying everything he could to get some from a 21-year-old girl. He really liked young girls like me—he told me so, said my youth made him feel like "the man." He truly thought of himself as a good Christian, yet he tried to use the Bible to trick me into giving up my (fake) virginity. And then he proposed. He asked me to marry him a mere two months into this torrid, not-really-so-much-love affair, because he couldn't wait to get me into bed. Me! I was almost flattered, but

I wasn't dumb enough to fall for it. I said no. In fact, when we met, he'd just divorced his first wife, who was also pretty young, maybe 29 or so. (Once, I called him to come get me from therapy and instead of Robert, his ex-wife picked up. She told me that I was too young for him, that he was still married to her, and that I needed to stop "playin' around with other people's husbands." Lord god, if that happened to me today, I'd be shook, but back then, I was half-crazy. With all of the gumption and stupidity I could muster in my crazy li'l head, I responded, "Cool. Tell him to come and pick me up in 45 minutes. Then you can have your husband back." Ugh! I wish I could be 21-year-old Gabby for just one more day! She had no fear! 34-year-old Gabby is scared of her shadow! Literally! I see my shadow and get spooked, like, all the time!)

Where's the middle ground? The middle ground between guys like Darryl and guys like Robert? I think that guys like Darryl are common when you're a round little fat girl and you're still young. In my early 20s and even in junior high and high school, guys liked me. Guys that had a real live crush on me but didn't want anyone to know. "Keep this a secret," they'd say. "I like you but don't tell anyone." In school, I just wouldn't get involved. I'd shy away from any contact with any guy, but I certainly refused to be someone's secret. I wouldn't be their shame. By the time I was 20, I was tired of being completely alone and decided that being someone's secret was better than being lonely. That's why I went along with Darryl and a few others whom I barely remember.

But while the guys my age were ashamed that they liked me, men my dad's age would openly hit on me, ask me out, and talk about how they needed a woman like me in their life. Like Robert. What the fuck. It seemed that guys who liked me secretly at 21 eventually grew up to liking me in public around 45. Did I just have to wait until my 30s to find some even ground where the guys I liked liked me, wanted to date, and didn't care what other people thought about it? How is that fair? How do I *not* lash out at someone who *isn't* ashamed to love me? Why was I embarrassed to be with Robert the same way Darryl was embarrassed to be with me? How do I figure out how to love and be loved in return, if it comes along with shame or embarrassment? Should I have been nicer to this gross old man who pretended to want to marry me? Should I have stood up for myself and stopped giving attention to this handsome but idiotic boy who just wanted my body? Maybe I should've been born in my 30s.

Things ended with Robert before *The Wiz* even opened. Whatever it was that we had lasted two and a half months, two marriage proposals, and one very cheap ring. *He* broke up with *me*. Not because I was horrible to him, but because he decided that if I didn't want to sleep with him or marry him, I was clearly a lesbian. SERIOUSLY! He said that! That logic doesn't track but OK. I felt nothing. I continued to bone Darryl for a few more weeks, until the end of the run of *The Wiz*. Then it was over. Soon after, Darryl got a girlfriend. She was a pretty Latina who was kind of dorky and not exactly skinny, but was agreeably *not* fat. I continued therapy and decided to forevermore throw shade at Darryl for the way I allowed him to treat me.

21-year-old Gabby feels like a different person. Like she's a fictional character from a series of books I read as a teen. She doesn't seem real, and she doesn't have much to do with me today, but I still feel saddled with her karma. With the remnants of her horrible logic and rash decision making.

Yes. Robert was terrible. Darryl was terrible, too. But I was the worst. Their karma is their own, and I'm sure they're both fine, but my bad karma is *mine*. Not just for my behavior toward Robert or Darryl but for my behavior toward myself. I knew better, but I let myself down. I really dropped the ball on myself. I didn't protect myself. Not my mind, not my heart, and not my body. The karma I get for not taking care of myself should be astronomical.

I don't know any more about relationships now than I did then. I'm still hopeless and hopeful at the same time. I have crushes on the wrong guys, and I'm like a scientist the way I try to collect any bit of data that will prove that the guy I like also likes me. And even when I do gather all of the data and facts, I'm often wrong. Or maybe I'm too abrasive and that scares guys off. Or maybe I'm not made to be loved in a real way. You see, the game has changed entirely now that I'm a successful actress (or whatever). When I was just a fat girl, guys that wanted me preferred that our interactions be private. But now, guys that don't actually like me at all want every single interaction to be as public as possible. "Hey, post that picture of us on your Instagram" or "Can I interview you for my podcast?" All of these favors spring over dinner and drinks, after weeks of flirty text messages. I think they like me, but they think I'm famous and useful. I somehow skipped over that middle ground where guys actually liked me but weren't ashamed of it.

How did I get here? What would my life be like if I weren't an actress? Would I have found my soulmate by now? Would I be married with children? Would I be happy then? I'm happy now. Is that other life a more fulfilling happiness? What if I had all of that? The soulmate, the kids, the family—but also, still, the loneliness? What if I had everything and everyone I've ever wanted, and I *still* felt lonely? Would I still blame some invisible force by the name of "karma"? Is karma even real?

Look, I didn't promise you a lesson at the beginning of this piece. I wasn't sure I would even *have* a lesson to learn here. This is me shouting into the void to see if anything shouts back. Nothing. I don't hear anything shouting back at all. Even here on this page, I am lonely. Maybe the lesson is to find the opposite of loneliness in my mirror. No matter how much has changed with me through the years, from 21-year-old Gabby to 34-year-old Gabby, one entirely consistent thing is that I was and still am Gabby. Perhaps karma isn't real at all . . . . Nope! I just hearted a shady tweet and immediately stubbed my toe. Karma is *real*, yo. But I'm starting to hear something yelling back from the void. Karma is real, but it doesn't apply to 21-year-old Gabby. I was 21! I was supposed to be a shitty person, then. Mission accomplished! I dated without any regard for whom I was hurting, or how *I* could be hurt. If I were a dude, I wouldn't even feel guilty about it. I might not even remember it happened.

Yep! That's the great thing about yelling into the void. Even if I have to wait a few days for it, I always get an answer, and the response I'm getting back is to stop. "Stop feeling guilty, you idiot! You were TWENTY-ONE! . . . Chill."

OK. Good lookin' out, void. I'm done.

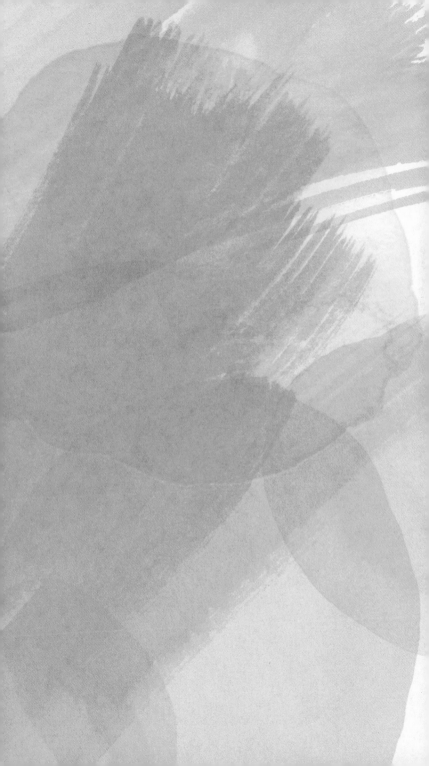

2 AM AT THE RAMEN SHOP AND I'M TRYING TO SAY I LOVE YOU

By Marina Sage Carlstroem

with your
tongue you slick the surface of your weatherworn lips
try to peel the mud off of my legs speck by tiny speck,
somewhere between your ragged cuticles and my icy palms lies
an entire power grid

one chopstick each
do friends share utensils?
you wring your hands until they
are dry of the tears you have brushed from my cheeks

why is it that you are always the one leaving early?

i give myself over to you in pieces
a coffee-stained book
a ticket stub
a secluded destination
explain me far better than my mouth can

you give to me in handfuls
fingers across my skin
a secondhand story
gray bubbles and sidesteps

the purple lights behind you whir loudly in our comfortable
silence.

you traced around your noodles for a moment
posing a question:
think of your day as
dollars and cents
who would you spend the most on?

i watch the whir of the lights become the static between two
pairs of hazel eyes. become the noodle trapped between two
chopsticks.
it is low and fuzzy in my chest like the overpowering bass in a car
i knew my answer before the final words passed your lips but
you know i'd pick a question mark over a period any day

then
you tell me that
all of your dollars and cents and noodles wouldn't add up to the
amount you spent each day
thinking about how my hair fell over my shoulder
the whir spreads across my skin and my lips give way to my teeth
for first time since the leaves fell

CENTRIPETAL FORCE

Melting into the universe with the singer-songwriter's greatest love.

By Mitski Miyawaki

It's the night before I hit the road again. For the next month I won't eat a real meal, I'll drive all day in a packed car, I'll forgo privacy and personal space, and I'll sleep four hours per night, all so I get to perform for an hour a day. A week after this tour, I have another, and another tour after that; I've been on tour for the past five years, all for my love of music.

Of course, I love music, I'm a musician. But music truly is the deepest, most complicated love I've ever known. It's my great romance, my affair of a lifetime, and my family, my sibling, and my own self. It's all of my loves, and my one true love.

I remember my mother would take little toddler-me to the park, plunk me on a swing, and as soon as she'd start pushing me, I'd start singing. I'd sing for as long as she pushed—we could've been there for an hour or forever, and I'd happily sing the whole time, all made-up songs with made-up stories, with no beginning, no end.

As with most childhood loves, I didn't become conscious of it until I got older, when you have to start naming your love and work for it. Kids don't think about loving something, they just do. So I spent my childhood in my head, singing to myself and noodling on the keyboard. Much of this had to do with my moving a lot. Almost every year I'd be in a new apartment, a new neighborhood, a new school, and often a new country with new cultures and languages I didn't speak. Everything I owned came with the proviso that I likely wouldn't have it for long, and I never had time to make friends. (Or perhaps I deliberately didn't make any, because I knew I'd leave again; a kid can only say goodbye so many times.)

But the great thing about music is that it's portable, and no matter what new city became my temporary home, I always had the music in my head to keep me company. I didn't need to go anywhere, I could just wander into the world that I'd created for myself, and it would be there waiting for me. I loved music because I needed it; music was an anchor in my otherwise floating existence, the one place where I could always return.

Things changed in seventh-grade choir, when I performed for other people for the first time, and my voice became something that was praised, and drew envy, and was sought after. For the first time I thought, *This is something I'm very good at.* Being good at something makes you feel necessary, as though you can contribute, and it switched on a light of a feeling in me, that maybe I had a reason to be there. And that's the blessing and the curse. To have a Reason with a capital *R* is what I think love is at its core, and having a reason is where all the strength and pain and beauty and hardship comes from. I found my Reason at 13, and every day since has been consumed by and dedicated to music. I wasn't from anywhere, and I certainly didn't belong anywhere, but being good at music gave me something to offer. Maybe I only ever loved music for what it could do for me, but then again, maybe people only ever love for that reason.

I looked around and asked myself, *How do I get my voice heard by more people? How do I make myself matter more?* All the women who were singing and being noticed were beautiful, so I concluded that I had to be beautiful, too. I began working out every day, I went through product after beauty product, I stoically restricted my eating. My every thought and action became dictated by whether something would make me prettier, because I thought being beautiful would give me permission to make music. I sold my body for a ticket in.

84

I understand how skewed this thinking is; how does being beautiful automatically turn you into a musician? I was a teenager, and there weren't any active musicians around me—or, if there were, I didn't see them in my rootless and solitary world. If I were part of a local music culture or had friends in bands, then maybe I would have had a less distorted view of a path to music. But from watching TV in my new house in another place full of strangers, the best answer I could come up with was that, to be a real singer, I had to be beautiful. I didn't know my own agency or how to change my life, only how to change myself. The only outcome I knew how to control was my own body's, and I thought if I looked like all those successful singers, then I could become a successful singer.

Yet all through my teenage years nothing happened, no mysterious musical entity discovered me, and I was just a friendless girl silently sweating at the gym. My love had betrayed me. I was spending every waking hour on appealing to music, to earn its love in return, by practicing piano and singing, or working out, or denying myself sugar or carbs; I was doing everything it wanted of me, and everything it wanted was so hard, so why was it denying me?

By then I was 18, and I'd graduated from high school a year early. I had endless time on my hands but nothing in particular I wanted to do, and I didn't know how I was going to live the rest of my life. So I went out a lot. One early AM I was very drunk again, and I was very sad but I didn't know it yet, and I got home to my room, plopped down at my keyboard, and started hammering at the keys, when a song spilled out of me, so urgently that I could hardly keep up. This would become my first song, "Bag of Bones." I'd written simple phrases of music before, but never with such intention. It felt like the world flung open its doors, like sprinting a full mile without ever taking a breath—yet also like dipping into a hot bath after a long day. It was a great scream, and for the first time I thought to myself, *God, I want to be alive.*

But I also understood then that I was doomed to love music and follow it to the end, because how can you feel the whole world pass through you like lightning, then go on with your life as if nothing had happened?

I kept writing, which let me let go of my obsessive beauty rituals, one by one. Now my body didn't have to be beautiful, because I could create beauty and offer it to the world. I had something I could really do now—that Reason again. Music was always my true love, but now I felt it was finally in this with me, giving to me and spurring me on. Music caused me all this grief, yet music somehow also gave me a way out of it.

I went to a music conservatory in New York, where kids my age were organizing and playing their own shows. I realized I could pursue music on my own terms. I didn't need anyone to "find" me anymore, because my songs could take me where I needed to go. I also realized that the only way to make music all the time as an adult was to make music my job. So I worked. I worked and worked, sent a hundred emails a day, said yes to the tiniest opportunities, and stayed on the road nonstop. After graduation, my life turned into either being on tour or being on a short break from tour, and during the short breaks I would crash and burn, never leaving bed but still emailing and answering calls until I hit the road again. I didn't hang out or "chill," because I spent any free time I had sleeping or working an odd job to keep going. Even when I found blank time to spend with friends, I would grow anxious within minutes, because I'd hear the music call me, telling me I'm wasting valuable time I could be spending with it instead.

I gradually got sick and exhausted, and I looked around and found no one. I had not only closed myself off from any opportunity for friendship, but I'd also landed a crowd of people who deemed my ambition ugly. As an Asian woman, I've found that people often think I should be grateful for any scrap offered.

When I give more than I receive, it's often seen as an equal exchange, or worse, that I've been done a favor. I was always asking for more, and moving on when I felt I wasn't in a reciprocal relationship, and in return I'd be called ungrateful, selfish. I find it interesting how often "selfish" is used to describe women who want more, demand more. Having to counter these aggressions, both big and small, over and over, made me incredibly tired. I thought music would give me a place to belong and make me happy, but all I could recall anymore was the hard ground I'd kept hitting as I ran after it. Why did I have to hurt so much over this love? If I quit chasing it, if I broke up with music, would I finally be happy?

But then right when I think music and I are through, it gives me that perfect show, those 30 minutes of a good performance, or even just three minutes of total contentment as I write a song that works. Instantly, everything and I make sense, and everything hard and hurtful I went through for those minutes vanishes. When music loves me back, I have the world at my fingertips, I become more than myself, I melt into the universe. This love may not be a stable one (it's certainly filled with hyperbole) and with every year of holding on I feel a bit of something in me falling away. And yet. Music is my greatest love, my oldest companion. It makes me feel alive, and it reminds me that I can't die yet, because I still have an album in me that needs to get out.

Here's what I always do at the end of each tour, in my first week back: I find a quiet place to be on my own with a piano or guitar, and I perform alone, for myself. Now that I'm the real working musician I always wanted to be, I spend most of my time performing for other people. So I stop and sing for myself, and for music, which has known me better and longer than anyone else in the world. It is a little embarrassing at first, like having sex with a partner you haven't seen in months, but we soon go over all our shared secrets, all the messes we've gotten into over our love, and I remember why and how much I love music.

ORÍKÌ FOR MUM

A praise song, a war cry.
By Sukhai Rawlins

You've been told you have your grandmother's eyes. You don't know if it's true, but you hope it is. Your mother doesn't have your grandmother's eyes, but sometimes these things skip a generation. Your grandmother is stunning. She wears her formerly cascading black hair in a fashionably short haircut. She has long fingers with long nails that never break, painted a smoky gray to match her hair color. Thin golden teardrops dangle in her delicate earlobes, their warm hues illuminated by chocolate tortoiseshell glasses that rest on the crook of her nose. Your grandmother has an impeccable sense of style you'd like to think she's passed down to you, but before her good looks you'd love to have her eyes. Her eyes tell stories. They dance when they're mad, they shout when they're sad, and they blink twice and shift from side to side when they're too mad and sad to shout or dance. Your grandmother doesn't need to talk; one look at those flashing brown eyes and you already know what's up. No one can really explain it—but that's the thing about magic, right?

You are the descendant of mystical Black women and your grandmother performs miracles. When she goes to the thrift store on Harrison Ave. with three dollars, she leaves with cashmere, silk, *and* discount Polo—bargains making her beam so bright, it's like she plucked the moon from the night sky and stuffed it into her Goodwill bag. Your grandmother is the kind of old woman television could never capture. The kind who wakes up with you before school on Monday when the sky is still a hazy blanket of blood and blue, swaddles you in the smell of sizzling onions and potatoes, and then swears at you for leaving your light on all night and running up her goddamn electric bill. She's the kind of woman who can't be contained. Whose loud voice is deliciously discordant, drifting through your kitchen and out the door, filling every crack in the sidewalk with honey; breathing daylight into dim and paint-peeled houses. Your grandmother is all knowing— she never went to college, but speaks with the wisdom of her past lives bubbling at her throat, springing from her lips like water through broken levees. On raw Boston nights when you forget what the sun looks like, you find yourself at your living room table, letting her words wash you in the dark baritones of healers and addicts, artists and thugs, lovers and warriors. Your grandmother speaks a color no amount of bleach could clean, a language your school will spend half a decade trying to scrub from your skin. Hers is a rhythm you recite to yourself at night when the darkness obscures your reflection.

Your grandmother is from the Wampanoag tribe of Massachusetts, an Afro-indigenous nation guided by matriarchs and wise women. You don't know much about her youth, except that she's the youngest of a family with 11 children, she was poor, and for a family of brown women, surviving in America was not always easy. Your grandmother tells you stories about being hungry and lining up with 10 siblings to take a bite out of a single thin sandwich her mother made. She tells you about living on a street with wild neighborhood kids and gambling with them over card games for M&M's and salt-and-vinegar chips. Your mother tells you stories about your grandmother's thoughtfulness. About how every cold day she would have a cup of hot chocolate waiting for your mother when she got home from school. Each story you hear about your grandmother informs your perception of her; every parable is a brick in the powerhouse you call "Mum." But there's one thing about your grandmother you don't learn from stories, there's something about her that—although never acknowledged—you know from a very young age.

Your grandmother will beat someone's ass. If anyone gets slick with her they're catching hands—end of story. No one is safe. Not the construction worker she hears catcalling you on your way to school, not her racist Irish boss at the veterans shelter where she works, and definitely not the white lady who cut you all in line at T.J. Maxx. You never see your grandmother fight anyone, but everyone knows she will, and those who don't know find out as soon as she looks at them. Not when she glances at them, when she *looks* at them. When she fixes them with a stare so deep they can see the glint of steel flicker behind her eyes. Your grandmother's gaze bears the venom of a spitting cobra and she passes it out with Jesus-like generosity—one look at those Ogun eyes and white people go running! After seeing your grandmother's face ablaze with that uncontained fury, it's like those people saw a ghost. The ghost of something they'd tried to bury long ago.

Your grandmother's stare isn't only reserved for her adversaries. You meet that gaze many a Saturday morning on her couch, when you're still wearing a bonnet, oversized T-shirt, and a night's worth of sleep in your eyes. When your grandmother sees you flipping through channels, she mutes the TV, drops the remote, looks you up and down, and says, "Girl, you are Drop. Dead. Gorgeous. And you better not forget it." Accustomed to her theatrics, you roll your eyes and laugh, but she doesn't. She's serious. She's more than serious, she's mad. Her words carry the weight of war, and she speaks them with a scowl on her face, cursing the name of the violent system that could call your brown skin, bedhead, crusty eyes, and morning breath anything less than magnificent.

When you are in seventh grade, you are taken from an all-Black middle school and put into an esteemed college-prep school where out of 2,500 people, you are the only Black girl in many of your classes. No one is ever prepared for racism. At 12 years old, you certainly aren't. But you are prepared to scrap with anyone who puts their hands on you. Like all Black people awaiting justice and change, you pray to the orishas Shango and Oya, so the thought of physically defending yourself against racists does not make you feel guilty, but it does deprive you of sleep. You think of your classmates' snide comments and furtive glances, and you can't get your mind to quiet. You wonder who will be the one to finally do it, who will be the one to push you to your limit. Will you get expelled for fighting them? If you do, will you still be able to get into college? In bed at night, you can feel your grandmother's presence in the room below you as you contemplate your fate. Would it be in class? Or on your way home from school? Maybe they'll corner you in the bathroom. No matter which, you are ready. When you look out of your window you feel like each star in the sky is an eye of your ancestors; lighthouses twinkling in the sea of heaven. You know they are ready, too. Each morning as you walk to school, their watchfulness is as sure as the sun; a bright spotlight shining on your forehead, making you sweat under its anticipation and glare.

On the day that Barack Obama is voted into presidency, the glare seems to lessen. Your grandmother cries tears of joy that morning, and as you walk into school and up the winding stairwell to class, it seems—for the moment—there is another Black person to hate, another Black person to root for, another Black person in the room, even if that room is all the way in Washington, D.C. For a second, it feels safe to breathe. In the suffocating herd of students shoving their way up the steps to homeroom, you saunter with a quiet tranquility. Putting your head down and grasping the banister next to you, you ascend the steps, when something wet on your hand pulls you from your thoughts. You look down at your fist, now coated in murky saliva. You are struck by the sheer amount of liquid; stunned at the length of the bubbly waste sliding along your knuckles and between your fingers. Adrenaline cuts through your astonishment. Gagging, you wipe your shaking hand on the thin cotton of your pants, the liquid's warmth seeping onto your thigh. Students in front of and behind you shriek with excitement, their faces contorted in a mixture of revulsion, entertainment, and glee. Over the deafening sound of your heartbeat, boyish laughter rings like a war cry in the near-stagnant crowd. You look up—ready to face your enemy. There are hundreds of them, thousands of them—the entire world has paused to relish in your panic, savoring the salt in your sweat and smiling at the smell of your despondency. You are frozen in time and space, and for a moment you are so overcome, you feel like you've left your body. Drifted and left it right there on the stairs.

Your vision blurs, you blink twice furiously, and all of a sudden your eyes dance. You don't realize what is happening until you feel them shout and look side to side, real slow. With a furrowed brow you stare piercingly into the crowd before you, dancing, shouting, side to side, dancing, shouting, side to side—and the bell rings, loud, clear, symphonic music for your dancing and shouting eyes. In what feels like seconds, the massive crowd dissipates. You stand there as homeroom begins, back in your skin, trembling. Tears roll down your cheeks and your once-clenched fists fall to your sides, arms dangling, palms open and empty, and your grandmother as far away as the president.

WHAMMO!

"A dream come true!" by ESME BLEGVAD © 2017 NYC

BEFORE I EVER EXPERIENCED HEARTBREAK I HEARD A LOT OF ABSTRA[CT] THINGS ABOUT HOW IT FELT. FOR ME PERSONALLY IT ENDED UP FEELI[NG] EXACTLY THE SAME AS A RECURRING DREAM I USED TO HAVE WHE[N] I FELL ASLEEP IN MATH CLASS. NOT, LIKE, EVERY CLASS-MAYBE 3 T[IMES]

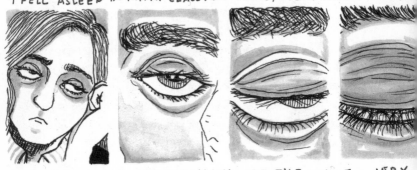

THE DREAM WAS ABOUT FALLING OFF THE TOP OF A VERY TALL BUILDING. IT WAS KIND OF MORE OF A NIGHTMARE BUT ALSO HAD A HEADY, DROWSY, CALM QUALITY TO IT.

Z

T WAS ALWAYS THE SAME, AND FAIRLY STRAIGHTFORWARD.
FIRST, I FELL OFF —

- AND THEN, FOR AGES,
I FELL DOWN, AND DOWN -

GAINING SPEED AND MOMENTUM AND A NAUSEATING RUSH OF ADRENALINE —

THUNDERING TOWARD THE GROUND WITH MY HEART IN MY THROAT AND MY STOMACH INSIDE OUT AND MY EYE-SOCKETS FLAPPING FROM THE SHEER INTENSITY OF THE PRESSURE — EVER GROWING! — OF THE FALL, AND ALWAYS AT THE SPLIT — SECOND MOMENT OF IMPACT:

I'D BE KNOCKED INTO CONSCIOUSNESS AND PHYSICALLY OUT OF MY OWN CHAIR, BACKWARD, BY THE FORCE OF THE CRASH, AND OPEN MY EYES TO SEE THE WHOLE CLASS LAUGHING AT ME FLAT ON THE FLOOR.

I FELT LIKE I KNEW THAT MY OWN BRAIN WOULD ALWAYS SAVE ME BY WAK
ME UP JUST - JUST!- AS I HIT THE GROUND BECAUSE IT COULD NOT ITSELF
PROCESS HOW INTENSE THE IMPACT WOULD ACTUALLY BE . I REMEMBER THIN
ING THAT IF ONE TIME I DIDN'T WAKE UP, THE DREAM MIGHT ACTUALLY KILL
ME I

AND SO THE POINT IS, ON THE VERY FIRST DAY OF MY FIRST REAL REAL RE
MIND - BOGGLING HEARTBREAK, I WAS SURPRISED TO FIND THAT MY FEELIN
GS WERE FAMILIAR, THAT I HAD BEEN IN THIS STATE OF RUSHING, HELPLESS,
UNCONSCIOUS MEGA-PRESSURE BEFORE : IN THE DREAM. AND I WAS NOW
AT LAST, IN THAT LAST SHRED OF A SHRED OF A SECOND AS I HIT THE GROUND
AND WOKE UP, SIMULTANEOUSLY, LIVING IT IN SLO-MO, INSIDE THE APEX.

I LIVED INSIDE THAT BANG TOO LOUD TO FATHOM . I FINALLY SAW
WHAT WAS ON THE OTHER SIDE. IT WAS VERY HD AND VERY. SLOW

T LIKE I SAID - I'D HAD THE DREAM BEFORE. IT TURNS OUT
AT I WAS WRONG, AND THE DREAM DID NOT KILL ME, NOT EVEN
EN I FOUND IT IN REAL LIFE. I SURVIVED THE FALL.

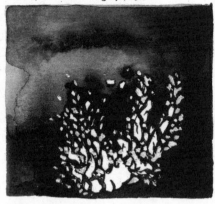

T THAT'S THE ONLY WAY I CAN DESCRIBE HOW IT FELT - I SAW
'SELF SHATTER. IT WAS AS HYPER-INTENSE AS I'D IMAGINED IT
ULD BE WHEN I FIRST HAD THE DREAM. AND WHILE I KNEW I'D

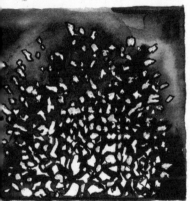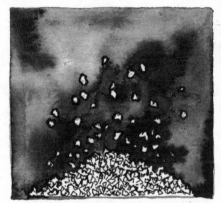

COME TO, THAT IT WOULDN'T LAST FOREVERMORE, I ALSO
KNEW I'D NEVER AGAIN WAKE UP ON THE CLASSROOM FLOOR.

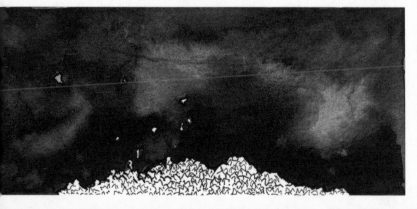

WILLIS

A devotional to dogs.

By Durga Chew-Bose

Late in *Rebecca*, Daphne du Maurier's narrator reflects on why dogs make us want to cry. Maybe, she wonders, it's how they express sympathy. So quietly, hopelessly, as if bound to—along with eating, sleeping, barking, and chasing squirrels up trees— some grave, too-clever sense of premonitory loss. Like Jasper, the novel's cocker spaniel, who recognizes something is off or altogether wrong the moment "trunks [are] being packed." When dogs see a suitcase or hear the hollowed-out, clumsy banging of one being retrieved from the closet, *they just know.* Their tails droop. Their eyes dim. Their paws drag. They sigh.

Dogs can tell which footsteps are hurrying to get out the front door, grabbing keys before remembering to turn off the lights, and which footsteps are merely puttering between rooms. They appreciate the kettle's whistle because it signals settling in. They might not like how the television emits rude, surly sounds, but they understand that its hold on you keeps you indoors. The dog will inch close, knead the couch's cushions until they are the correct snug shape, or curl up on the floor. "A heartbeat at my feet," wrote Edith Wharton.[1] Because really, all the dog wants is that you stay. *Why leave? Why leave me?*

1 From "In Provence and Lyrical Epigrams," *Yale Review* vol. 9 (January, 1920)

Aren't I enough, they seem to ask when they tilt their heads and park themselves on door thresholds. When they raise their eyebrows—like floating, puppet eyebrows—as if to say, *Goodbye? Again?* What's worse is when they give up on you before you've even pulled on your boots. They'll give you their backs or amble to another room, and suddenly, your life screeches to a halt because your heart shoots up into your throat. You want to chase after them and say, "I love you. You know that, right?" Sometimes, I don't even say, "I love you." I think it. I'll think it loud. Though I always say, ". . . you know that, right?" It's the reassurance that needs repeating. Loving my dog is not just love, but specifying love's bumper. Love plus love's insurance.

Because dogs are sensitive to the air that sparks around a family running late to their dinner reservation, maybe to somewhere fancy, or to an appointment where the dog isn't invited. They know which coat you keep for long walks in the park—that vast expanse of green or snow, sticks, smells, and other dogs like Bernie, Jack, Hugo, Bear.

But as du Maurier notes, when the house empties and becomes still again, the dog is exposed to that terribly human sentiment: loneliness. All he can do is wander back to his bed as the car pulls away. Actively, dutifully waiting is a dog's purpose and burden. He sits perched by the window or near the front vestibule.

The dog's chin is, perhaps, the most despairing of his features. The way he rests it on whatever surface suits. Other than his paws, the dog's chin is his most worn-out—one can't even call it part, but—trait. Characteristic. The dog's chin brings attention to his mood. The dog's chin is where he stores his demeanor. His exhaustion. His blues. And where he chooses to rest it, that, too, conveys attitude; a sense of humor. A punch line.

But when he's alone and everyone is gone, and I worry that daylight has waned before we've made it home in time to turn on some lamps, the dog's chin is terribly sad. The chin is him, inconsolable. His chin is hope disappearing. And sometimes I want to trace every surface where he's rested his chin, because one day, he'll be gone, and I'll want to look around and see chin prints. Chins remembered. Heartbeats at my feet.

AFRAID OF LOVE

By Ana Gabriela

I'm afraid of things
I can't even understand
I'm afraid of you
walking around there.
I can say "I'm OK"
when you seem to care
is not that I don't love you
is just that I don't want you to hurt.
I want to tell you things
that I see in my dreams
but every time I try
I just want to disappear.
I tell myself if it is OK
is it OK to love you?
is it OK to be afraid?
I'm not good at many things
but I wanna tell you today,
that I want to explore the world with you
and I don't want to be afraid
when I hold your hand.

QUICKEN THE SENSES: A CONVERSATION WITH MARGO JEFFERSON

On developing and celebrating your instincts.

By Diamond Sharp

I first discovered Margo Jefferson's writing through her memoir, *Negroland*. I connected to her cutting descriptions of living with depression and mental health issues. Her impressive career—which has spanned over four decades—has served as inspiration for me. She is currently a professor at the New School and her memoir, *Negroland*, was released in 2015.

DIAMOND SHARP **What role does love—self-love, romantic, platonic—play in your practice as a writer?**

MARGO JEFFERSON What role doesn't love play? I'm a critic, and that means I'm always defining myself—my sensibility, my prose, my feelings—by what I love. By what I dislike or hate, too, but you can't think about what you hate without trying to define, ever more closely, what you love and why. Romance quickens the senses—that's always good for a writer. My closest friends are my best readers, and often my muses, too. Family? Katherine Anne Porter wrote [in her essay "Reflections on Willa Cather"], "Childhood is the burning fiery furnace in which we are all melted down to essentials . . ." Family is your first experience with that essential primary material.

I had the pleasure of seeing you in conversation with Morgan Parker and other women writers on the topic of depression. What approach do you have to writing on depression?

There's no one approach to writing about depression. I'm just finding the ways to approach it—I'd never written openly about depression before I wrote *Negroland*. There, I treated it as private, psychological material, as social and cultural material, as a retreat (an angry respite) when life felt unjustly overwhelming. I'm interested in its obsessive quality—depression can be addictive, a kind of lure. And more and more, I'm interested in how quietly, stealthily it affects one's everyday tastes and needs. How could I write about it undramatically, even benignly? Is that possible?

What encouraged you to begin writing criticism? What tips do you have for someone starting off?

I started by reading the criticism of writers I admired—novelists and poets as much as full-time critics. This encouraged me, because it excited me. It fired off my intellectual and emotional synapses. It quickened my sense of how my mind could work. That's a good way to start. But apart from that, always pay close attention to what excites you in any and every way. What books, what movies and TV shows, what music, what visual artists and performers? Surprise yourself. Follow the work, the artist; keep notes about it, describe it and make it come alive. Then scrutinize your own reactions and motivations. Notice what you like, even if people you respect call it "trashy" or "uninteresting" or "offensive." Notice what you're trying to like *because* there's a cultural consensus about it. What are you insecure or snobbish about? And play with language as you describe and evaluate! And remember that evaluation needn't be a fixed, lofty judgment. It can be a collection of thoughts-in-progress. It can be a series of questions.

Your conversation with Jenna Wortham and Wesley Morris on their podcast, *Still Processing*, after the 2016 election, was both incisive and comforting. What advice do you have for those deterred by the election results?

Read widely and think hard. Take action—there are all kinds of organizations and outlets. Let the people you trust and love help give you courage.

Your memoir, *Negroland*, was an informative read to me, as a fellow Chicagoan. Can you talk more about what influence Chicago, and love of home, has on your work?

I haven't lived in Chicago since I left for college in 1964; I've only visited. That means it's a site of memory and history for me. My childhood and adolescence, of course, but even more the world that my parents, their relatives, and their friends made. It's American history and literature in action for me, a story that I'm always rereading. It's a historical narrative, it's a multigenerational family saga; it's a drama and comedy of manners.

What is the most important thing you've learned during your career as a journalist?

Don't get too comfortable with what you do well. It's easy to be praised for one voice, one approach that becomes your signature—your *brand*. There's nothing wrong with that, but don't settle for it. You'll start boring yourself.

What have you learned about writing from your students and from the act of teaching it?

When you teach writing, you have to give a clear shape and language to your practice. And you have to ask if your practice suits the work of each writer you're teaching. It doesn't always—how could it?—and so you have to know enough about the craft of writing to propose other methods. That's useful. It makes you more intelligent about writing in general. And it can offer you ways to work you hadn't thought of, ways of shaking free from old habits. My students belong to different generations. Their cultural frames and references aren't mine, and often they're fascinated by different writers and aesthetics. They'll recommend works I don't know. This can be humbling, and even embarrassing—it's hard for teachers to give up the omniscient narrator role. But on the whole, it's fun.

BEFORE I STARTED WRITING THESE THINGS DIRECTLY TO YOU

Two jokers in love.

By Tavi Gevinson

Chipped front tooth, mod mop of black hair, a lack of facial awareness that means his smiles are big, goofy, and free (borne of freedom, freedom-inducing, and given freely). I have fallen in love with faces that were perfect blank slates, big glass eyes that popped in and out depending on the mood, that granted attention if the weather was right. The magnet then was the possibility of discovering what was behind the face: How could anyone possibly be so perfect that their mouth didn't curve beyond the realm of indifference, beyond the privacy of the emotions I'd hoped they were fostering for me, somewhere among the silence? What was going *on* in there?

With him, I don't want or need to *know* anything; just meet him on the plane where he seems to be gliding through whatever is happening in this moment, looking outward and not watching himself, no more *crane* shots, just accepting each new event as soon as it begins and the previous has passed—kissing and clasping hands, saying "hi" out of nowhere and once accidentally in unison, the unspoken but mutual fear of cliché when he says something like, "It's dumb, but you're very pretty," and I can't say anything back because I'm still working through the fear of looking dumb myself, and besides, silence is the best descriptor for all the things he is; silence, I hope, tells him I'm still processing, that I'm in awe; that I'm Agnes Martin-ing it for now. Silence, maybe, or the last thing I said as I fell asleep the other night, which he informed me of in the morning, and which has become a mutual substitute for all those other mushy words: "I hate you." I hated him so much last night when he put on one of those doo-woppy Christmas songs and sang along very softly, matter-of-factly, almost like a nursery rhyme, an inch from my face, and it was so impossibly sweet that I was, I believe, frozen, and when I listened to it alone this afternoon, my cheeks and temples caught fire, and I had to put my face in my mattress, and I sort of blacked out before realizing I was crying. He skates on the rings of Saturn. He makes every love before this seem so stupid, so sad. He said he used to get in trouble with girls, in high school, for keeping his eyes open when they were making out: "I was too in my head. I was just looking around like, *Where* are *we? What are we* doing? And then they would get mad, and I'd be like, Sorr-y, *Dana!*" Sometimes, when both our sets of eyes are open while we are kissing or just very close, he puts his hands around our temples to block out everything everything everything else and says, "Protective shield!" I told Celia and she went, "Like a View-Master!" Sometimes they also feel like binoculars. Or a kaleidoscope. It's all lovely. And the chipped-tooth grin.

I feel bad that I just stare, that my stare sometimes can't grin.

"What's wrong?"

"Nothing! Why? What?"

"You look sad."

"I'm not!"

I'm in awe! I will explain this to him . . . at some point. Today I texted him the Ralph Wiggum valentine that says, "I Choo-Choo-Choose You"—baby steps. I am aware of the impending ironies, I will try very hard to not become the people I've previously dated. I just don't trust words a whole lot, and wonder if writing this, too, takes the

114

air out of the whole thing, like in the Chekhov story "The Kiss," where the sad loner shares the story of an improbable romantic encounter with his male colleagues and, upon hearing it out loud, experiences the whole thing as woefully insignificant. Similarly, I giggle a lot when I am around him, and when he asks what I'm laughing at, I pull out some event from recent memory, realize halfway through that it's only funny if you were there, and cut myself off to sigh and then wail in agony, to mime hanging myself or banging my head against the wall, and he laughs harder than I was originally, and I laugh harder than he is now, and the ways in which life and connection and simple communication are so fucking *hard* become wildly funny, and I lose it even more in this absurdity-induced mania. Are my jokes funny? It doesn't matter! The great thing about sense of humor—much like, I guess, love—is that it's not about taste or quality, the way people talk about having good or bad taste in movies or clothes or what have you: It's what literally makes you laugh the most, so it can never be wrong. Rationalizing is no longer necessary. I feel no pressure from within to understand why it "works" and say things to friends like, "It's great because he works in X industry but isn't Y type of person!" None of those things matter; if you're good enough at words, you can make anything sound like a sensible partnering. If you're good at arguing, you can defend a sad relationship like a very skillful lawyer. In this case, I don't need words, because I have the feeling: inarguable, indisputable, its own creature.

THE HEART ATTEMPTS TO CLEAR ITS NAME

By Bassey Ikpi

let me remind you why i was placed here
not to ache or welcome hurt and break
you have accepted this too easily

clear my name

i'm here to move blood
to pump and pulse and remind you living
you are living

i'm doing my job

despite the thing that curdles
there is still oxygen available
i will not own this

will not let you

say it hurts
there is no shame in this
say you wish to curl into yourself

claim the aching disappointment
but blame the spleen

your useless gallbladder
when was the last time your appendix owned anything?

i can not own this

i have kept you moving
despite the ache
the tragic need to lie down and force paralysis

who kept pace

i did.
and pulse.
it was me.

i allowed you movement
when you were ready
when the time to mourn has lifted

you will forget me again

but where was your gorgeous brain, while i toiled?
probably thinking the unimaginable;
fooling you into believing that this could kill you.

i kept pumping

showing you that i would never fail you
sending you a praise song through your veins

i love you most of all

you think i'd break for another?
think i would ache for anyone

other than you

clear my name

write of how i've saved you
how we walked through this life
the days i was the only one listening

where is my poem

i'm tired of the blame
the heart aches
the heart breaks
the heart fails

the heart tries
the heart lives
the heart pumps
and pulsates
and carries

i make sure you don't remain tethered
when this clears
when the eyes you never consider enemy
show you the truth

perhaps you will thank me then

until then, i will continue to move this blood
to provide this body oxygen
you continue to mourn

i will be here when you wake

SELF-ACCEPTANCE

On playing to your strengths.
By Sarah Manguso

I would have been happier in my 20s and 30s if I hadn't thought that in order to be a real writer, I needed to write a very long book. Even after four, five, six books, I was still revving the engine, getting ready to write my long book, using a voice and style and mode I never wanted to use but felt obligated to. I thought of myself as provisional, a placeholder, the self I would remain only until I magically became the self I aspired to be, with different interests and a different sensibility. I lived in a permanent state of aspiration. How would it have felt to accept myself as a more or less fixed entity? Doing that seemed like giving up, like a decision to stop breathing.

I started writing so many long books, and as I began each one I felt that I was about to become the person I was meant to be: the author of a very long book. I also felt, just as immediately, that I was completely uninterested in writing it.

Soon after he turned a year old, my tiny son's proclivities emerged. He preferred vegetables to meats, mud to paints, and he still does. Before he could stand unassisted I'd bought him an easel. Years later it stands mostly unused; he prefers his rock collection. As people who have known a person from birth understand, his personality is bound by a collection of fixed tendencies and attributes; it is not a rough draft to be developed and improved into some other painting, carnivorous child.

To my surprise, soon after my little baby became a child, complete in himself, I realized that my daily experience had taken on an unfamiliar calm. When my oldest friend fell apart after yet another perceived public humiliation, I no longer wished she would, by somehow erasing all memory of her childhood, change into someone no longer so highly susceptible to shame. And instead of becoming fed up when my husband was depressed and couldn't be reasoned with, I felt myself detach from the contest of reasoned argument and tried instead simply to comfort him. Without my noticing, I had suddenly become better at accepting other people as they were.

This new skill has also drifted into my self-appraisal. For the first time, in my 40s, I have come to wear my jeans and write my pages with a measure of equanimity, to live without a constant background hum of self-dissatisfaction. A certain inner conflict is in the process of disappearing, a conflict I never quite knew was there. Perhaps this is a common experience, attendant to raising children or arriving at midlife; perhaps it is so common it isn't worth mentioning. Whatever the case, I wasn't expecting it. It occurs to me that perhaps acceptance is a widely applicable skill, like reading.

I no longer expect to become a person who writes a very long book, but that concession doesn't feel like a failure; it feels like a context within which many things are yet possible. I've come to understand that some of the things I'd told myself I'd do someday are pipe dreams. Giving up on pipe dreams is not resignation; it is giving up on an imagined momentum toward some improbable end.

Play to your strengths. This is good advice often given; it is also a fairly good insult. My mother-in-law once said to me, very gently, while I was fretting about failing to fit into anything off the rack in some clothing shop, "We all work with what we have." She was tiny and slender. Her kind, well-chosen words hit me right in the heart, truer than some line about how being tall is good, which a less thoughtful person would have immediately said, followed by some self-deprecating line about being short.

I dreamed and dreamed of waking up in a different body, of having written a book I would never write, and then I stopped dreaming. Further transformations are coming—I am not yet fossilized—but I no longer think I'll achieve selfhood only after some impossible transformation, a transformation into someone else.

HOW TO CONFESS YOUR CRUSH

Be active in your admiration.

By Krista Burton

"I have to tell you something: I have a crush on you."

It was still warm out, an October day with green trees and green grass and a breeze that ruffled the lake's surface, like the water was getting a noogie. Ellie* and I walked the trail around the lake a lot—we'd spend an hour and always slow down when we passed the volleyball area with the shirtless college dudes.

My heart was pounding. I did it. I had just told Ellie.

She turned to me and smiled. "I know," she said. She reached down, took my hand, and kissed it, like a fairy king offering a peasant a blessing, like the most natural thing in the world would be to kiss another girl's hand.

My heart exploded.

My god, I loved Ellie. She was so beautiful to me, and when you talked to her, she really listened, as if you were the best and most interesting part of her day. She wore big gold hoop earrings and zero makeup, and she was so entirely herself that had she not existed, there would probably be a black hole in the universe shaped precisely like her body. Ellie was too cool for me—a shy Mormon baby from Wisconsin in thrifted clothes that didn't fit right—but the minute our freshman English composition class

* Name has been changed.

had let out on the first day, she had asked me if I wanted to go get coffee, right then. Like *Oh, this is how people make friends.*

Now we were juniors, walking around the lake. I'd loved Ellie the entire time—even though I'd dated a bunch of people in the years between. And now I'd finally said so.

"I love you, Krista." Ellie still had my hand, and swung it as we walked. I was so happy, I couldn't believe I'd waited so long to tell her, now we'd be together, she'd felt the same way the whole time, too.

Ellie put her other hand over mine and stopped walking. "I don't love you like that, though. Just as a friend. Who I really love."

Ellie's eyes were warm and wary. She'd done this before. Everyone was always falling in love with her. Once, a well-dressed 50-year-old woman at a bar had come over to us like she was in a trance, only to give Ellie her card and tell her she'd like to take her to dinner. I was not the first to see Ellie, or to be sure I was in love.

Ellie put her arms around me. "I don't want to lose you as my friend."

She walked me home, and I didn't call her for six months.

If you've ever had an intense, *life-altering* crush on someone, you know how romantic feelings toward that person can consume your thoughts. You also maybe know the anguish of *not* knowing. How does your crush feel about *you*? Do they know you love them? Maybe they have a secret crush on you but are too shy to tell you! Or maybe they don't know you exist, ahhhhh.

Telling someone—whether it's a close friend you've known for years, or a stranger you just laid eyes on at a diner—that you like-LIKE them is a hard thing to do. The situation is fraught with so many variables, and it could go in so many ways. Your crush could be thrilled and feel the exact same! Your crush could be blindsided and not know *how* they feel, because they'd never thought about dating you! Your crush could be happy and flattered; they could be annoyed because this happens to them all the time and *omg can't they just have a friend?*; they could be potentially interested but then not feel any chemistry with you; they could even be shocked or angry if they feel your crush threatens them or your friendship. Telling someone you like them seems like such a small thing, but, in fact, it's brave and nerve-racking and, often, absolutely terrifying.

And that's why everyone tries to get out of doing it. Who wants to stand vulnerable in front of another person, exposing their innermost feelings and being open about what they want? Why don't you go ahead and crack open your rib cage, and let your crush see your beating heart with their name tattooed on it?

Yes! I'm here to encourage you to do it. Crack open that rib cage. Show your heart. Learn from me, Rooks. Don't spend years of your life wondering (agonizing) if your crush likes you—tell them! No matter the outcome of admitting your feelings, you'll *know*. It's hard to move forward with someone who doesn't know you like them. It's also hard to move on from someone if you think the two of you still have a chance. Don't hang around in crush purgatory: tell them, loves!

THE ACTUAL TELLING OF THE CRUSH

Only you can know where and when you want to tell someone you have feelings for them. Maybe you hang out together alone all the time, and you could tell your friend privately during one of those sessions. Maybe you don't know your crush well at all, and you feel more comfortable sussing out how they feel about you in a public space or through a trusted friend. (This is a legit and time-honored way to find out if someone like-likes you, y'all.) Maybe you chat or text with your crush but don't know them well in person, so it would make sense to convey your feelings through the screen. Maybe you want to write a cute note and stick it in their locker and then ignore your crush forever after in the hallways, hoping they approach you, now that the ball is in their court. There are a million sweet, worthwhile ways to tell someone you like them, and doing so only *takes* about 30 seconds to a minute.

Which is why we're not talking about HOW to tell your crush they're your crush. Once you've decided to do it, it takes no time. What we're actually discussing is what happens *after* you tell your crush you like them. Because that's where things can get hairy.

As far as I know, you have three possible outcomes after you've said your piece, and all of them have infinite variables for how your particular story with this person can go. Let's get into it, shall we?

1. Reciprocation

Reciprocation is the option you're probably hoping for when you tell your crush you like them. Your crush likes you back and tells you so! OMGGGGGG YOUR CRUSH LIKES YOU BAAAACK GAAHHHHHHH. Telling someone you have romantic feelings toward them and having that person say they have romantic feelings toward *you*? It feels like winning the damn lottery. Like: *WHAT ARE THE ODDS, UNIVERSE?* How wild is it that in all the world, the person you've been thinking about constantly has *also* been thinking about *you*?

In a classic reciprocation situation, you want to date each other and be together and swap special secret animal nicknames and lie under trees in parks just looking at each other's perfect faces and marveling at how you both like each other so much.

I hope this is what happens for you. I'm rooting for you and your crush. I hope y'all get to date and fawn all over each other. I hope it's wonderful! And works out! And is everything you wanted!

2. Complication

Life has funny twists and turns, friends. SO FUNNY! Very few situations are 100 percent straightforward. Here are some ways things can get confusing with your special someone:

- So you tell your crush you like them, and they tell you they like you back ... but your crush is already dating someone. Whom they *also* like.
- Maybe your crush likes you, too, but just got out of a nasty breakup and doesn't feel ready to jump into something new.
- Maybe you both like each other ... and one of you isn't allowed to date. At all.
- Maybe your potential relationship would be queer and one of you is struggling with what that means. Or one of you is an active member of a religion that frowns upon or forbids homosexuality.
- One of you could be too busy to date, with school and homework and sports and an after-school job and a kid brother to watch.
- Maybe one of you likes the other *way* more, and the other person is mostly interested because they're enjoying the attention.
- Your crush? The last person they dated was ... your best friend.
- Your crush *is* your best friend, and even though

you both like each other, you are terrified of losing your bestie if this doesn't work out.
- You and a close friend have the *same* crush, and now said crush is only interested in *you*.
- Hell, maybe you and your crush are *both* dating other people, and you're all in the same friend group. Fun!

Any of these scenarios can happen when you tell someone you have feelings for them. Sometimes you can like someone, they can like you back, and it's not possible to be together yet . . . or at all. That can be really hard, and just as heartrending as finding out your crush doesn't have feelings for you in the first place. Waiting sucks. Having to be patient and/or mature about a crush situation is difficult. The thing is: Once you've done the work of putting yourself out there, you can't control what happens next. Learning to come to terms with whatever situation comes your way after you've done your part (being vulnerable and stating how you feel!) is part of Getting Grown.

Whatever happens with your crush—whether y'all end up getting together, or never do, or experience something in between—it'll work out, Rooks. Promise. I'm going to give you some more ideas on possible scenarios, and ways to deal with what happens.

3. Rejection

I hate that we have to talk about this, but we do. I'm sorry. You might tell your romantic interest that you have romantic interests and . . . find out that they don't. Maybe they'll be gentle. Maybe they'll flat-out reject you. (They better not laugh, or I'll come and find them.) No matter how it goes down, it turns out the answer from your crush is "no."

"No" is valid, loves. People are allowed to reject you. "No" hurts, and "no" is also something we need to accept and learn to live with. At least you have an answer! It's clear, and you no longer have to agonize over whether the person you're obsessing over likes you. They don't. It sucks. But now you can move forward with your life.

I know that sounds a little cut-and-dry, as if it's so easy to turn off your heart. But ya gotta do it when it comes to rejections. And when it comes to moving on . . .

Do it, bbs! Do what you need to get over that person, whether it's cry or talk it out with friends or go running on a country road while scream-singing LeAnn Rimes's "How Do I Live?" over and over. Get all those gross feelings out of you! You need to *heal*!

Try to be good to yourself. Find some things that you like and do them. Throw yourself into your social life; try something new and scary that you're interested in (for me, the scariest thing on earth is improv classes), and focus on living your life! Who needs your crush? Not you!

There's no real way to get around it, though—what you most need to get over someone is time. A moment will come in the aftermath—days, weeks, months on—when you realize, with a jolt, that you haven't thought about your old crush in a long time, and that will be startling and also feel good. You may even think, *I can't believe I liked them so much!* Or think it's funny you believed you were *in love* with someone who didn't love you back. Time makes sharp emotions feel blurred and fluffier; it lets you breathe and examine a situation with new eyes.

Until then, here's what you don't do:

Don't hang around hopefully (because you've memorized your crush's schedule), thinking they'll change their mind. Don't keep stalking their social media. Don't "check back" with your crush a few weeks or months later, and don't flirtily text them or send them funny/adorable snaps designed to make them fall in love with you. Why? Because you don't need the person who has rejected you. This is a person who has seen your innermost desires, seen you at your *most vulnerable*, and said, "Nah." This person is not who you want in a dating partner. If they change their mind and want you later (not unheard of), they know where to find you and you can let them come to *you*. Otherwise, if you keep up the flirty snaps and sweet-yet-definitely stalk-y behavior, you're mentally keeping your crush around, and it's harder to let go.

Rooks, when Ellie rejected me, I lost my breath. I thought I could not actually continue to live. When I woke up the next morning, all I could think was, *She doesn't love me*, and it was this hideous heavy feeling, like a warty troll sitting on my chest. But here's the thing—life works out the way it works out, and eventually, it was OK. *I* was OK. I met someone in the months afterward who made me forget loving Ellie so much—I had a *new* crush, and it was wonderful and reciprocated. We had gross secret animal nicknames for each other and a journal we passed back and forth and we spent hours sitting under trees in parks, marveling at each other's perfect, perfect faces. I spent a long time loving Ellie, and I still love the *thought* of her—but reality? Reality turned out great.

Tell your crush you like them, my loves. Be active in your admiration, and be ready to handle the consequences. You can do it!

LIVING BY THE BLADE

Arthur, again and again.

Writing and illustrations by Annie Mok

In T. H. White's reimagining of Arthurian myths, the 1958 novel *The Once and Future King*, White delivers his version of classic heroes: Arthur, normally portrayed as a brave lad, is under the thumb of his brother, and is a "hero-worshipper." Lancelot, usually notable for his beauty, is described as ugly. There are also, as my friend Lee pointed out, multiple scenes of Lancelot and other young men wrestling sweaty and naked. Lee calls *The Once and Future King* "the sad gay knights book."

I read these stories originally in *King Arthur and His Knights of the Round Table* by Roger Lancelyn Green. The book cover is in a vintage video-game, pixel-art style. I remember playing Game Boy Advance, and seeing art like that always makes me think of those worlds—full of transformations and magic.

In one story by Green, Arthur throws his old sword into a lake, and Nimue, the mystical Lady of the Lake, gives him in trade the mystical sword Excalibur, which only Arthur can wield. The exchange calls back to many fairy tales and myths in which the giving transforms the gift, coming back to the giver. This archetypal story is detailed throughout different cultures in *The Gift: Creativity and the Artist in the Modern World* by Lewis Hyde. Hyde describes this loop in the connection between making an artwork and giving a gift: "Having accepted what has been given to him . . . the artist often feels compelled, feels the *desire*, to make the work and offer it to an audience."

Myths hit at my heart with what filmmaker Guy Maddin called "melodramatic truth" in an interview with film critic Robert Enright for *My Winnipeg*: a heightening of reality that speaks to an emotional and psychological core greater than a more straightforward rendering might. These tales of swords and sorcery, dragons and transformations, reveal something to me beyond this vale of tears in which we live. As I am a trans woman who's undergone transition, the magic that changes a person from one form to another resonates with me. Names hold power in Arthurian myths, and T. H. White plays with these names cleverly: When he's young, Arthur is "the Wart," and he becomes Arthur. Guinevere, Arthur's queen, becomes Gwen. As I became Annie.

Like many ever-evolving stories, the myths of King Arthur—maybe even the man himself—might have come from a historical source. In one tale, a sword is buried within a stone that no one can pull out. *National Geographic*'s "The Truth Behind: The Legend of King Arthur" traces it to its possible beginnings: A swordmaker creates a sword by pouring molten metal into a mold, eventually pulling a sword from a stone. I love this link to creativity, as I often feel that every story is in part about the art of storytelling itself. Each story reflects the conditions under which it was forged.

I'm writing my own graphic novel now about King Arthur; nearly all the characters are trans and of color. But even as I write it, I struggle with the weird ideas and misogynist aspects behind it. Arthurian myths are concerned with chivalry, but contain brutal attitudes toward women: for example, Guinevere and her romantic relationship became a scapegoat for Mordred and other knights to defect from and declare war on King Arthur.

I'm thinking of my approach as hopefully a kinder one; like T. H. White, I want all the villains to have souls and interior lives. Lancelot will be a trans woman and Arthur will be a trans man.

Everything falls apart in the stories of King Arthur. Even during the prosperous times of the Round Table, Arthur keeps in mind the wizard Merlin's premonition of the battle that would tear his kingdom apart. This echoes the knowledge that we all must live with, the idea that one day we will die.

Yet in the end of Green's version, Arthur is taken to Avalon, a mystical island in which he seems to go into a deep sleep many lifetimes' long. For he is the once and future king, prophesied to return when England needs him. This seems to reflect the question of one's soul, whether it lives on, and the multiple incarnations of the Arthurian myths themselves. The chivalrous code—that a knight must be Good and self-sacrificing—is alive in pop-culture mythos like Batman and *Star Wars*. Arthur is always returning.

The King Arthur stories are often violent, but the violence enacted by the knights is never random, always pointed at men, often men who terrorize women. I believe (I think, I hope) in the concept of restorative justice, but I also believe that safety is sometimes only enacted through violent measures. I don't believe in that "kill your local rapist" jean-jacket-patch rhetoric, but I like reading fictional stories wherein men who fuck with women are killed.

I'm left with a pile of books. A pile of books about loyalty, beauty, and friendship—dripping in racism and misogyny. One part of the King Arthur myths will stay true to its heritage: I'll transform them again in my version.

ONLY SHALLOW

To know and to Know another.

By Britney Franco

Start with a dream. On some craggy protrusion of rock, some distant moor, anywhere where the barking cold becomes romantic—we stand as if never separated, but with the knowledge of our reality. Between us lie the Akashic records of our union: everything that has ever been thought, said, woven, drawn. Neither of us moves toward them, but their air calls to me, a siren song that only I can hear. I think of all that goes unuttered whenever I pass you in my translucent shroud, dulling every sign of life so you won't be tempted to steal more of me. "You know," I say, "my old twin died."

"I know," you say. My mother's death has been a specter throughout our liaison. I have talked about her endlessly and dutifully, the miserable daughter searching for another half to mimic and fill the space she left.

"You felt like the new one, but something was always off. Every time I stressed our sameness, I found more errors." I look straight at you for the first time since our tradition of staring contests ceased, and, surprisingly, you match my gaze. "I always knew how it would end."

"Then why did you do it? Why did you keep going?"

I continue to look at you. I wake up before I get to see who loses.

We establish a difference in knowing, unsaid. To know someone is vast territory, but limited to acquaintanceship, a surface level.

knowing and Knowing you has been a practice of mine. To Know you has been to go from watching you try to rewind my broken cassette player in physics class to sitting in your room as you rewind the sounds that your brain has told you to throw into the atmosphere, looping and twisting them for hours until they become a mold of your heart's contents. I take a certain pride in Knowing you, one that I cannot fully explain except that I admire the ideal of you that I've crafted in my mind, and the slivers of your basic principles that resonate so heavily with my soul. You despise words, but something is interesting in everything you say. I think when I listen to you. You do not feel like someone who belongs here, and I admire that you are so good at recognizing this and quietly imposing your own world on everything around you. As we grow closer, you show me your art and your music, and although I cannot find myself in it, I am excited by the prospect that someone else likes to channel their energy into spreading pieces of themselves around. It doesn't matter if I like it. All that matters is that everything made is a kind of Horcrux, something you've produced with a piece of yourself hidden away in it as an F-you to the fact that one day, the rest of you will be gone.

Knowing makes me the girl with the most cake. "You are the knowing one," you tell me. Eventually, it becomes a sick joke, one that you either do not recognize or pretend to be unaware of. (Over time, I lean toward the latter.) I gradually begin to understand the plays on my narcissism that you are so fond of, and the sickly umbilical cord between my obsession with self-observation and the need to scry myself in another, announcing, "Here— my twoness is a sign that my presence is valid enough to be replicated—I am not an error—"

In ninth grade, I do not know you as anything more than the casual presence in two of my classes and, on occasion, in the back of my mind. I do not know why you exist in the second, but perhaps it is because you are someone I barely know but could see myself

Knowing, based purely on superficial similarities. They mean almost nothing, but they are a shock to me because I am not yet used to relating to people. I make you a mixtape that feels like the final concrete slab in my catacomb-construction kit, convincing myself that it will be a good idea once I get past the shame. I hide it in a book at home (thank god) until I find it and promptly throw it away.

Dublin, 1980, *Rest Energy*. The artists Marina Abramović and Ulay are each leaning against their own walls of air, all of their stability lying in the bow and arrow suspended between them. Ulay grips the string attached to the arrow, Marina holds the bow. The piece lasts for about four minutes. Later, in *Walk Through Walls*, Marina writes: "This piece, with a big bow and arrow, was the ultimate portrait of trust . . . We were both in a constant state of tension, pulling from either side . . . if he slipped, I could be shot in the heart."

For all the months that we Know each other, the image of the three—Ulay, Marina, and the loaded bow—haunts me sporadically, giving me a soft kick when I am looking for holes to poke into this newfound happiness. Would you hold on to the arrow until the end? My answer (or lack of) makes me shiver.

Maybe I am asking the wrong question. Had you bothered to pick up the bow in the first place? Were you ever really holding on?

I wish I could tell Marina that even if the arrow hits her heart, she will have to continue to live afterward, using the blood that escapes from her chest to mop up the friendly fire, gathering torn tissue and arteries under a looming failed regime.

We walk into the graveyard after our time on the hill and I tell you that it is my first. My mother does not have a headstone; I have never had a reason or opportunity to visit this land of the dead. The flatness of the sky is all I can focus on, past the identical nature of the stone seraphim levitating over our path.

Mausoleum passing. "Why do some of them have tiny houses?" you ask. I love your questions. "What a waste of space. This is why I don't want a grave. I don't want to be a waste of space."

"I don't want a funeral. I don't even want to be buried. But I also don't want to be cremated." I think about how I never thought my mother would lose her body. "Honestly, when I die, they can just throw me in the trash." I like the way we talk because there is truth in all of our jokes.

We reach a crossroad. "Which way?" you ask. Eenie-meenie-miney-mo, yes or no—that way. I point and we walk. "It's another hill," you say; you skated the last one we were at.

"I'm gonna do it," I say, resting my board down.

"No, I don't want you to get hurt." You said this last time, but this road is worse and the cracks are unforgiving. I'll be fine. I'm willing to risk my skin for a thrill. I feel you watch me as I go.

"Love doesn't even exist, it's just a chemical created in the labs of DuPont . . . it was an accident!"   —Dale Gribble, *King of the Hill*

"Like dancers, none of us gets over that figure we see in the practice mirror: ourselves."   —Hilton Als, *White Girls*

As we get closer, we begin to talk about twins. I have always feared and loved the idea. A running joke I had with my mother was asking what she would do if she had two of me. "Oh no," she'd say with widened eyes, "one is more than enough." I loved the idea of being too much for others, and just enough for myself and someone else. In old movies and shows I watched as a kid, there were always twins whose dual effect was cataclysmic, strong enough to bring about the Rapture. I believed that I could find that.

My obsession with twins is based in my obsession with

myself, and cutting apart my history to understand why I turned out the way I have. It is so much easier to see who I am when I am looking away, analyzing my traits in the reflective surface of another. But the biggest appeal is the unity it offers, something that transcends friendship and dating and any other socially constructed closeness.

June and Jennifer Gibbons, aka the Silent Twins, were identical twins in Wales who thrived/suffered from their closeness and only communicated with each other in the form of their speedy patois-idioglossia hybrid. In his 2000 profile for the *New Yorker* on the sisters, "We Two Made One," Hilton Als states: "Their lives were the tale of a whole that divides and cannot be made one again." The isolated nature of their relationship was intensified by their childhood move to a community "known for ... spectacular racism," in which they had to be sent home from school early every day. The two were catatonic when kept apart; they wrote a series of novels throughout their adolescence and committed a series of crimes that led to their institutionalization for 11 years in Broadmoor Hospital, a high-security mental-health facility. Eventually, June and Jennifer decided that one of them had to die for the other to live a full and socially acceptable life; Jennifer offered to be the sacrificial lamb.[1] In 1993, shortly after their transfer to Caswell Clinic, Jennifer could not be awakened. She had died of a sudden inflammation of the heart, with no evidence of drugs or medication playing a role.[2] June went on to give a few accounts of their life to the public, and then moved into a house near their parents.

You also become fascinated with June and Jennifer after I tell you they'd been the inspiration behind one of our favorite albums, *Jenny Death* by Death Grips, as well as the concept of twin talk, something I find very comforting. I have a booklet full of silhouetted bouquets, and I begin to write different quotes and words

1 From "Inquiry Into Death of Silent Twin," *The Independent*, by Jason Bennetto, 1993
2 From "The Tragedy of a Double Life," *The Guardian*, by Marjorie Wallace, 2003

of ours in it, crossing out the italicized *Romance* on the cover and writing CRYPTOPHASIA.

I lose the booklet in school on the last day of junior year, and one of my administrators tells me that it is gone forever. "You're definitely not gonna find it," she says, shaking her head. "Don't even bother looking." I'd had the smallest feeling—what I soon acknowledge as intuition—that the booklet was not going to last and I'd found slight relief in that.

(This is another time in my life in which I continue to ignore an ultimate truth that I have predicted for a while: how the course of this experience will go and how it will end. But my biggest flaw has always been putting my feelings ahead of everything else, the antithesis to the Spartan romanticism I observed as a child. My mother let her well of love flow into me, but she was adamant about staying behind turrets when strangers came calling. "Don't pay attention to crushes," she'd told me from the start of my elementary years. "Focus on yourself. None of the other stuff is important. You come first." The exercise in self-love was crucial, but it closed all the doors to the outside that I desperately wanted to fling open in the throes of some passion.

(I am afraid to not experience what it is like to allow someone to have this kind of intimate presence in my life, even if the future hurt is looming and glaring at me from its unknown distance. I hold her words parallel to everything that happens with you, slowly understanding her intent through the veil of my own Via Dolorosa.)

We begin to develop our own meanings for words, an expedition you lead. Even with something as fluid as language, something that I am so used to and enamored by, I find myself daunted. I hate the feeling. I try to read your mind; we learn how to talk without speaking, something I am (positively) daunted by. As a writer, I have always aimed to encapsulate things as best as I can with the words I have gathered, but I also think the ultimate expression arises from communication that transcends the limits humanity has imposed on itself. There is something to be said about the simple joys of having someone to acknowledge as a sort of Other Self; on the other hand, the extreme focus on tying together all the strands of our twinship forces a close eye on our dissimilarities. The search for same becomes more biting than the coexistence of our differences. I pretend I am not losing myself.

I like looking in your eyes as I try to dissect them. I like looking in your eyes as I try to dissect me. I like looking in your eyes as you dissect me, whether you are trying or not.

"If you die before me, I'll cut off my left hand and put it on your grave. But if I die before you, you have to write in print for the rest of your life."
"Really?! You'll cut off your left hand?"
"No . . ."
"Oh . . ."

"At first Jean-Michel thinks this is funny and puts some of her words in his paintings. Then he tells her to shut up."

—Jennifer Clement, *Widow Basquiat*

The striptease of our divide begins a few days before I turn 17. We do not talk daily anymore, nor do we see each other.

We are in the park with three of my best friends. You are talking to the one I have known the longest, inseparable in the way I usually am with her, or with you, at times. "Sometimes I just get bored with people," you say to her. You look up, and your eyes flick over to mine. They land hard. "It happens with everyone. Some people more than others."

Over the hours that tumble out after the Big Reveal of your growing apathy, you do not speak to me. Not once. I wonder how long I have ignored the tumor; flashback to my earlier denial of my mother's own failing system. Defeat feels more sinister the second time around. I am the knowing one, and yet I have allowed my knowing to feed off of itself rather than weaponizing it. I sit to the side, wondering if I am a masochist or a pragmatist for continuing to stay with the group. You are the center, a welcome change to your hovering, but I am receding into myself. "Look at them! I've never seen him look so happy," one of my friends giddily says. I stare at her because I already have your image in my mind. You are in a slight embrace with the longtime best friend. I have seen you look this happy before.

Part of what draws me to you is your equation of what others would call infatuation or deep affection with sickness. It is how you first tell me that you like me: *My stomach dropped in a new way when I saw you—I feel sick and I don't know why—you make me feel sick—you're making me sick.* I revel in being an infection.

I listen to you speak when we are in the park with my friends, a blend of phrases you have thrown at me in the past but are reclaiming now. You say to my best friend, "You make me feel sick." She doesn't get it. She shakes her head. "You make me feel really sick sometimes," you try again. It is the first time I resent the desire (here, a need) to vomit around you; I wonder if it is too late to grab back the reins to the pit in my chest. I don't have a high-enough platelet count to build an effective wall, other than the passive silence I've allowed to lie on me throughout the day. I think about my mother, the death announcement, the subsequent months of survivalism, and then I say to myself: *This is the worst thing I have ever experienced. This is the worst I have ever allowed myself to feel. You make me sick.*

It is my birthday. You and the same trio of my best friends move throughout my apartment and the surrounding area of my neighborhood. You alternate between almost dead and active, but the latter is only in interactions that are not with me. A string of men harass me on the street, and you say nothing as I scream. I am on edge the whole time, juggling the invasion of your gaze with my own internal presence. My friend gives me a card in which she jokes about beating you up and I ask her if she will do it. You say two sentences to me during the entire day. One of them is to ask me if I am OK at the end of the night before you get on the train. I want to laugh, but I am a fooless with nothing left to offer but my zeroness. I skate away.

Junior year: We are at the Whitney during the tail end of winter, when it is on the brink of breaking but still dedicated to its obstinance. Our project for art history requires us to go see the Frank Stella retrospective, which we both ridicule. "You don't have to pretend to hate it just because I do," you say. I am offended, but I do not say. I pretend to write something down in my notebook.

Later on, we move to other floors of the museum. As I flit from piece to piece I see you roaming in my periphery, glancing between me and whatever I am in front of. I enjoy knowing that you are there. Things begin to offer me new meanings. I am wittier in my analyses, or at least I try to be. I begin to Know what is before me.

We are awaiting the elevator. "Have I ever showed you my mom?" I ask. You shake your head; instantly, I am excited. I pull out her picture from the bend of my journal. She is smiling in the snow, a beam beneath her big flannel and denim.

"She looks so happy," you say. "It's a shame that someone so beautiful had to die."

The sentiment is strange, not in its nature but because it was a thought I'd had before while looking at pictures of her. I'd found it funny because it sounded like something I could hear you saying. I do not tell you, because it is enough to know.

"I always feel bad about stuff, like all of it's my fault," I say.

"Maybe it is. Maybe you're the one that killed your mom."

You chuckle a little, then continue to laugh to yourself. Instantly, I am transported to some bad dreamscape that I want to deny as reality, even though you are here and you are real, and the light enshrouding us has not been generated by my mind. The most absurd part is that I have had an underlying fear of this moment for a while, but it was so specific a terror that I did not bother to prepare for it, deeming it irrational. I say nothing. The elevator arrives and we ride it to a different floor. Cindy Sherman greets us wearing three different faces. We continue unfazed.

There are only a few things that I can remember immediately after the car hits me off my skateboard and runs over my leg: *This is real—my older cousin's phone number—I have to call you—getget-getgetgotgotgotgotbloodrushtomyheadlithotlock—the pain is here.* I am hypnotized by the swelling beneath my tights, but I do not want to cut away at the cloth swaddling it because I fear facing the wound head-on. It is the most I have ever felt with my body.

I am transported to the emergency room by an EMT who holds my hand and prays in Spanish with me. It is a glimpse of purity, and I know that if you could see it you would laugh and say, "To pray is to admit defeat." Your atheism tickles my soft spots—warm discomfort. I have a growing list of all the instances of beauty and dynamic life I have witnessed that would earn a hearty scoff from you. I have touched the skeleton of the cosmos time and time again, collecting the chips it drops into my palms. It feels good to have my own vault, but I wonder . . . what does it mean if you cannot understand why I pull what I do from the world? You think I am simple, or silly, or at least questionable for looking beyond my own air, for calling energy God, for seeing more potential for the soul than rotting in a box. What does it mean if you laugh at my reasons to live?

I tell the nurse that I must call my older cousin, whom I've already dialed, and try to reach you instead. I know that you will not recognize the number and will not pick up until the last minute; you greet strangeness like it is garmented in reaper attire. I am right. "Hello?" you mumble. I smile at the haziness of your voice.

"I got hit by a car and I'm alone in the hospital," I say. I find myself grinning even more, not because it amuses me but because I am assuming your position. Mine is too much to handle. Too much victimhood to carry.

From my journal:

> 8/2/2016
>
> I called ___ from the ER and it was strangely unsatisfying in a way I've come to expect but didn't want. It was a Very Us talk, where I told him my swelling was oblong when he asked what it looked like and he laughed because my family wasn't here and I laughed with too much braggadocio over my bones being too strong. We talked about X-rays and whether or not I could keep a copy of mine and he talked about how he got one of his hand and oh no, my doctors are back, bye bye. I feel sick. I never thought I'd get hit by a car and have the worst thing about it be no one caring.

It is good to have your voice in the small room, but I am dulled by every response. I have nothing to do, but I choose not to explicate tidbits of speech. You are always telling me that I am stuck in words . . . time to unstick.

I call you again later. The routine is the same. You pick up as I begin to dial my best friend. "Tell me a story. I have nothing to do and my family still hasn't come." You have nothing. I hang up and drag myself to my room, where my cousin eventually joins me.

Around 1 AM, she and I are talking about what to expect once the doctors come to splint my broken ankle when I look through the window that stretches across the room. "Holy shit," I let slip. I am in more shock than I was when the car slammed into my body. You and your family—whom I've grown close to—are approaching. I know that it is not an illusion because my fentanyl has not been administered yet. All of you offer smiles for my gaping mouth.

Spending time with your family has been the most tender part of our non-relationship (a union with no name, which becomes even more pronounced every time we are referred to as friends). No matter what spaces have sprouted between us, your parents— especially your mother—have been there for me, ever since I met them and told them about life since my mother's death.

I watch your mother and my cousin—a mother to me in her own right—meet for the first time, and I feel like I am holding the sun in my chest. You smile at my swelling and then at me.

More journalspeak:

> That was one of the most wildest, most beautiful, and pure experiences of my entire life and I'm still in shock. I forgot that a hospital room could be so full of warmth and love.

You finally watch *Natural Born Killers* after I watch your favorite movie, *Akira*, twice. "I hate it," you say.

"Are you serious?!" I ask.

"No ... I'm just messing with you. I love it."

A few days later, I am away on a school trip. It is deep into the cut that dawn has made on the day and I am still awake in bed with my roommates, on the phone with you about the snake rings that Woody Harrelson's and Juliette Lewis's characters exchange in the movie during their highway marriage and are to never take off. (In one scene, Harrelson's Mickey Knox notices that Lewis's Mallory has removed her ring and goes berserk. "If that ring pulls out every hair on your head, it stays on. If it tears out my eyeballs, it never comes off. Every great thing we do starts with these." He puts his hand with his ring over hers.

"Do you know what ring avulsion is?" *No, but I have an idea, what is it?* "It's this thing that happens when people can't get a ring off and it tears their finger. I'm afraid to wear rings. If I weren't I would get the ones that are in the movie."

When I am home, you give me a new word that I put into my CRYPTOPHASIA booklet: ouroboros (per *Oxford Dictionary*: "a circular symbol depicting a snake . . . swallowing its tail, as an emblem of wholeness or infinity"). You constantly find ways to unknowingly regurgitate symbols and associations that I have made throughout my life into our union: snakes and their tangles, twins, living iconography.

It is far past midnight. It is strange, because this is one of the first times I have ever had a full conversation with you, and this has always been such a murky yet revelatory crevice of the day for me. It is so intimate that I usually spend it alone.

"I'm listening to one of my favorite albums," you say.

"What's it called?"

"*Loveless*. It's by My Bloody Valentine."

I put it on. "Only Shallow" is the first track. In the dark, I begin to cry.

The next day, I am still thinking about that initial sound, the one that crashed into the base of my belly, throttling me from the inside. I want to know if it is about what it makes me feel. I find a forum discussing the lyrics and scroll, unsatisfied. One comment catches my attention; it contrasts the violence of the instrumentals with the softness of the vocals, proposing that the former represents the "rough, meaningless sex" one might have with someone they don't care about, and the latter is a reflection of love one-upping lust, making a physical experience go beyond flesh.[3] It makes sense. But I am thinking not about sex, but

3 From jblondin, http://songmeanings.com/songs/view/62059/?&specific_com=73014914652 (2005).

feelings, and so the next comment resonates even more: "sounds to me like he's referring to a hollow relationship. like, the people are passionate about each other but don't truly love one another (in the mirror she's not there). i dunno. i mean the title IS 'only shallow'."[4]

I hope this isn't only shallow.

We once were two
We two made one
We no more two
Through life be one
Rest in peace.

—*a poem by June Gibbons,*
on her twin's headstone

4 From jawamachines, http://songmeanings.com/songs/view/62059/?&specific_com=73014892996 (2005).

MONSTER

By Florence Welch

So you start to take pieces of your life

and somewhat selfishly

other people's lives
and feed them to the song
At what cost
This wondrous creature
that becomes more precious to you
than the people that you took from

How awful

To make human sacrifices:
a late-night conversation
a private thought
all placed upon the altar,

but you can't help making a monster

THE JEALOUS TYPE

How to be fair—to yourself, and others.

By Amy Rose Spiegel

Everyone, at some point in love, is "the jealous type." Despite its rampant popularity among *llllovers* throughout history, romantic jealousy can be flummoxing at best and HEART-WORLD-CONSUMING at worst. To begin this piece, which aims to dismantle jealousy's wack and harrowing influence, I've listed how this strain of possessiveness asserts itself as thoroughly as I can. Here's what I came up with:

- Romantic jealousy means loving something and wanting to protect (and aggressively defend) it.
- It isn't *envy*, quite: You don't want to gain what someone else has. You want to keep your person closer, tighter. (The problem: Even if you love reciprocally and respectfully, no one is entirely *your* person.)
- It means you think of love as personal property that, if not adequately guarded and surveilled, can be taken away from you.
- It is a very painful kind of vigilance.
- It is induced by little things as much as larger ones, and by things that would surprise the person you love, if they knew. (Until you tell them: They don't know.)

- I hide jealousy because I don't want the other person to hurt, but I'm hurting.
- Jealousy is both mundane and illogical—banal and batshit.
- I get angry at my jealous self because I place the other person in a position of responsibility for *my own* feelings of injustice or betrayal, which can be unfair.
- I get angry at myself when I'm jealous because it places my supernatural love squarely on Earth: It proves my love can be exposed to the trivialities and trials of historical/archetypal love as everyone has known it. It proves my way of loving is not unique or even rare, and so, it is unsafe—if I'm jealous, it means I'm dull. (If you particularly identify with this thought, I prescribe the semiotic heart-manual *A Lover's Discourse* by Roland Barthes, which maps the banality of jealousy with orienting precision.)

Grim list, I know. Or, it seems that way, without a reminder that the underlying fact throughout is: All of these feelings are BEYOND NORMAL AND INEVITABLE. You're not a bad or weak person for thinking anything in key with this list. You love your person, and romantic jealousy is an unfortunate offshoot of that love. What matters most is deciding how you act on it. (In most cases that don't involve a person actually double-crossing you, this will not include yelling, demanding access to their passwords, or suggesting that you "collaborate" on their personal journal entries.)

As a young buck, I refused to acknowledge that my feelings had a "jealousy" setting at all, let alone that my brain was frequently, readily tuned to it. I believed—and still believe—that jealousy is, most of the time, a fruitless, one-sided, self-hating, and stunted state of mind. Unfortunately, that doesn't automatically convince me that my romantic jealousy is just irrational fear. But realizing that I'm responding to a partner's normal-ass goings-on jealously does help me recognize how to move forward. I can't always avoid it; I *can* manage and mollify it.

When I was 13, I started dating Andrew.* When I met him in the halls my freshman year, it was immediately clear that we would be together (which we were, for all four of the years I was in high school): He was smart, funny, and sweet, and he had great taste in the *Garden State* soundtrack—while also, like me, disliking the actual movie! Perfect. We spent our days side by side, sharing the earbuds for his iPod (this was forever ago—imagine me reminiscing in a craggy grandma voice), working on the school newspaper, running for student council, and competing on the mock-trial team. So, too, did a girl whom I would come to resent, be wary of, and eye-roll at: Jane.*

Freaking Jane! She was Andrew's friend from grade school, and she—damningly, I thought—liked all of the same stuff we did, so she was always around. (*The nerve!!*) Even though the shared tastes that drew me to Andrew might have, logically, also made me want to be friends with her, I saw her presence, and her good rapport with Andrew, as a threat. The two of them drove me up the wall every time they spoke to each other. In these moments, my face became a strange Halloween mask: the classic costume of "person trying to look cool and *fine with it!!*, who is instead smile-grimacing with her eyes narrowed so hard she almost strains a muscle."

One day in mock trial, Andrew affably pointed out how amusing it was that, when speaking numbers aloud, Jane always said *zero* instead of *oh*, like how you'd say the letter—this was because, she insisted, "*O* isn't a number, but *zero* is!" Boy, did he *love* that. Another was her strange pronunciation of the word *correct*, which

* Names have been changed.

sounded, Andrew glowed, "more like cricket." (These are great examples of the small, situational facets of people that only become magnified in the context of high school classrooms.) I couldn't fathom how these traits qualified her allure rather than how totally irritating she was; simultaneously, I busied myself by vengefully trying to devise my own winsome way of emphasizing syllables. Thrill at the heady powers of untrammeled teenage jealousy, my sweet comrades!

For those keeping score: I froke out and felt undervalued and threatened because Andrew passively appreciated something about how another human inflected her words. OK . . . also, I noticed him glancing at her chest once. BUT HEY GUESS WHAT, that is also fine: Committed relationships don't deactivate attraction to other people—yours or your partner's—and as long as you're both respecting each other's boundaries about what is and isn't cool in that regard, there's really no problem with that.

Unless you are teenage me or someone like her, that is! My jealousy of Jane introduced a maelstrom of other insecurities: other things I wasn't—I started to ruminate over all my perceived bodily and sexual failings every time Andrew and I boned—and the things I didn't even know I wasn't! It was KILLING ME. But in conversations with friends, I refused to believe I might be jealous—after all, I wasn't setting mandates about whom Andrew could or couldn't talk to, or otherwise freaking out *at* him. Jealousy, I thought, was forged only with words. I thought that *saying* I wasn't the jealous type was enough to make it true, like a political bumper sticker "absolving" me of the responsibility toward any real activism, but for my heart.

With this label stuck proudly in place, I began acting like a miserable, myopic private eye, spying on my own relationship, looking for any possible fissures, and, when I found none, inventing them. We texted all day, every day, and if Andrew didn't get back in touch with me, I worried that it meant he didn't like me anymore. I sulked without any explanation when he hung out with other girls socially, even in groups. I sometimes checked his phone while he showered or slept, despite never, ever finding anything. I could barely watch TV with him, lest a model shilling toothpaste cross the screen and stoke my feelings of inadequacy.

A private sense of wrongness pervaded every time I semi-successfully pretended to myself that I wasn't prying or otherwise behaving jealously even as I was doing it. I hated being jealous so much. It felt awful, like I was dumb. The jealousy I felt was borne of hunting, externally, the tricky sadness emanating from inside, which I also couldn't name for fear of having to deal with it. Many parts of my younger life made me feel worth-free—I thought that, because I wasn't perfect, I was useless—and I refused to be satisfied with the evidence that someone electively liked me. I rewarded that kindness by questioning it constantly. If I'm in a certain headspace, I have a tendency to find things wrong. If something feels good, I will biopsy it in the hopes of exposing a single diseased cell, which will then infect the whole.

I think these very ethical and levelheaded moves make clear that I didn't really like my boyfriend all that much, given this unkindness toward him, nor did I like myself. If my own behavior has been recently dicey, or I don't like a current something about myself, I am twelve-thousand percent likelier to feel romantic jealousy. (Of course: There are times when people's actions might lead to these feelings without your willing participation, and it's important to know the difference.) That's ungenerous to my partners and myself.

Once I had established myself as prone to jealousy without actually copping to it, any not-great behavior on the part of my boyfriends could be excused (by them) as my own neuroticism. In trying to hide my jealousy from Andrew, I succeeded only in emphasizing its prevalence and its pettiness, and where there once hadn't been any real problem, now there were plenty. That's kind of what happens when you mistreat someone and drive them away from you with mistrust. Andrew, noticing how agitated I'd become if he mentioned that he'd hung out with a group of friends that included *a girl, any girl*, started hiding his plans from me—and spending more time with one girl in particular, on whom he developed a crush. Pushing back against feeling any natural/mild jealousy was a detriment to me not only because it made me feel worse, didn't work, and sometimes backfired more profoundly, but also because it set me up to never admit to feeling double-crossed or hurt when it came to being mistreated in reality.

I do better to think about the problem behind the "problem": What am I feeling paranoid about when I doggedly refresh the "Following" tab on Instagram, looking for "deceit" that isn't there? (Again: It wouldn't be deceptive if, in fact, my person *had* liked another girl's vacation photo.) What am I hoping to find out about myself or the person I love, as I do that? And snooping *is* hoping to find something; against all logic, the more painful it is, the better. Will it mean I am right when I don't consider myself pretty or interesting? Is my self-worth that flimsy, that easily destructible? It doesn't have to be, but remembering that takes a bit of work.

My jealousy was fueled by the boring conviction that someone else's attention was all I had, or could have, going for me. As with so many other backbiting feelings in life, you can alleviate jealousy by making other, more productive things about yourself more immediately true. By focusing out instead of in, jealousy shrinks. Here are some steps to help you reduce it:

1. If you are on the internet, get off of it. This includes anything happening on your phone.
2. Drink a glass of water.
3. Write down your feelings, and, as my friend Durga Chew-Bose wrote in her book *Too Much*

and Not the Mood, realize that they can end with the two words ". . . for now," which suggests, to her, "the give and grace of compassion." To wit: "I feel like my jealousy about the way another girl pronounces the word 'crreeckt' means I'm dull and plain, for now." "For now" is a promise: You will not always feel this. An after exists.

4. Think about the aspirations and hopes you have for yourself outside of romantic or sexual candidacy. Fill your whole body with the idea that you are so much more than the current thing you're bugging out about, not "for now," but *for always*, and it will outlast this temporary crisis. If you find yourself becoming jealous over something that doesn't even follow those standards to begin with, it's useful to remind yourself that that's not who you are.

5. Decide whether to tell your person how you're feeling. If it is based on actions they have taken, like concealing information or being too blatant about other attractions for your comfort, and you want to stay with them, you need to have a conversation. If your jealousy, instead, lives only in your own fears, that's something you might feel more able to work on alone first. Consider what is most helpful and progressive, and act accordingly.

It's no surprise to me that these feelings melted when I decided I was determined not to feel so much spite and frustration for the rest of my life. (That hadn't worked out so hot, anyway.) I wrote with consistency; I dressed and looked how I wanted to instead of how I thought I had to in order to measure up to the

Janes I fretted over; I loved politics (and hated them even more vehemently) and acted on those feelings. I made friends. After Andrew and I broke up, I dated a higher volume of people who were nothing like one another, which also reaffirmed to me that there's not one right way to be romantically or sexually viable. There isn't an ideal. There's just you, enjoying someone else, and vice versa. *It can feel good.*

If you are feeling like you are less than you want to be and like you are less than others could want to date: I am sorry about whatever made you feel that way, but you don't have to keep feeling that way anymore. Also: Don't read anyone's diary, as a rule. You are going to be OK!

FROM SPARK TO BONFIRE

The iconic actress on where love lives.

By Marlo Thomas

To define love is an impossible task. Because love is a feeling, and feelings defy words.

It reminds me of a wonderful scene in the play *Children of a Lesser God* by Mark Medoff, in which James, a teacher at a school for the deaf, tries to describe music to his new student, speaking and signing his words at the same time.

"You see, music is..." James falters.

"Music has a..." he tries again.

Finally, he takes a deep breath, and this time as he speaks, his hands explode in movement, and he bounds from one end of the stage to the other, as if conducting an invisible orchestra.

"Music starts with pitches. Sounds! High and low. And each one has its own emotional life. And you can play them on different instruments—trombones, violins, flutes and drums. And then when you combine them and play them together...It transcends mere sound and speaks directly to your heart."

That is how I feel about love. Its definition eludes us, even as it speaks fluently to the deepest part of our hearts.

One of the great myths of life, I believe, is that in order to feel love—to be happy—we must focus on the things that we want, and then pursue them with all that's in us. The perfect job. The house by the beach. Fame and fortune.

But what I've learned through the years is that love doesn't live there. It lives in who you are, and who you share your time and life with, and in the way you give your own love.

It's like watering a plant. If you tend to a plant with attention and care, you will see leaves slowly begin to sprout, and flowers blossom.

This is the very essence of love: we receive it by giving it.

Love is also in looking for—and finding—the bonds that take you outside of yourself and connect you with your community. When I was 16 years old, I went door to door in Los Angeles, asking people to sign a petition for gun control. I was passionate about that issue—I still am—and by the time I was done, I held in my hands reams of pages with signatures. I'll never forget the deep sense of belonging this gave me. It had nothing to do with the "things" I wanted from life at the time—the fantasies of one day becoming an actress, or getting good grades in school, or finding the perfect boyfriend. It was about doing something that I believed was right, and it spoke to my heart in a deep and wholly unexpected way.

I believe that this is the truest path to finding love: by looking for the inner spark that illuminates the corners of your soul and turning it into a bonfire.

And, if you're lucky, you find love in your work. I've been very lucky in that. I love my work as an actor, and it's a feeling that's been with me my whole life. I loved to perform even as a small girl, and I would put on little shows at home. We had this closet in my bedroom, with a wide sliding door. I would step into the closet and close the door, and then my sister would announce, "Ladies and gentlemen, Miss Margaret Thomas!" Then she'd slide the door open and I'd pop out and sing a song.

Kids' stuff, for sure—but the feeling I had of loving what I was doing as I stood before my family, seeing them smile and clap, has been with me ever since.

So I continued to perform—in high school, and then in

college—and when I made acting my profession, I discovered more and more that the truest reward was not the rush of excitement I'd feel seeing my name in lights, or getting a nice review in the newspaper (though both can be gratifying!), but the knowledge that I'd built my life from something I truly loved.

And that inspired me to devote myself to performing even more. Acting is a craft, and so I sought the masters—Lee Strasberg and Sandra Seacat and Uta Hagen. The most important thing they taught me is to live honestly onstage, or in front of a camera. Acting isn't about saying the words of a character. It's about connecting to their heart and their pain and their joy. And in every part you play, you reveal another part of yourself to yourself. It is always an exciting adventure.

"It's in the doing, not in the thinking," Lee would say. And the doing is what I love. Whenever I walk into a theater, two hours before curtain, and look out at the empty seats in the audience, knowing they will soon be filled with people who have come to hear our story, I feel more than just lucky. I feel that I am where I belong. I am home.

Of course, my work shares its place in my heart with many other things I care about: inspiring young people to reach for their dreams; supporting St. Jude Children's Research Hospital, which my father founded; sharing my life with my husband, who himself defines and redefines love in new ways every day.

Like James, I continue to listen for the music of love, and to celebrate it. That is a journey I wish for everyone.

As told to Lena Singer

DAY ONE

OUR HOTEL ROOM HAS ONLY ONE BED AND NO SOAP.

WE SHARE THE BED.

I usually get self-conscious about sharing a bed with anyone.

I'M WORRIED I'LL SNORE OR KICK IN MY SLEEP...

I DON'T FEEL THAT WAY WITH B.

what do you wanna watch?

BEFORE WE MET IN PERSON, I'D WORRIED WE WOULDN'T BE ABLE TO GET OVER THE INITIAL AWKWARDNESS, BUT THERE WASN'T EVEN ANY ICE TO BREAK.

...Newman

Oh my God

WE SIT IN BED AND WATCH SEINFELD LIKE WE'VE LIVED LIKE THIS OUR WHOLE LIVES.

HE LEND ME ONE OF HIS BUTTERFLY CLIPS.

ONLY AFTER I PUT IT ON DO I REALIZE...

ME

B

HOW SIMILAR WE LOOK.

We are the exact same person...

Isn't there a trope about queer people dating their lookalike?

oh my God, shut up!

Looks aside, we really are similar. We share similar family experiences, and have the same sense of humor and taste in gifts.

Thank you

The whole day we spend walking around town, we finish each others sentences, and sometimes communicate only with our eyes.

We buy shower gel at CVS.

DAY TWO

we go out to breakfast

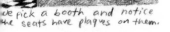

One says tom cruise and the other says rosamund pike.

we pick a booth and notice the seats have plaques on them.

oh shit! I know the movie they filmed here!

I watched it with my grandma, it sucked!

I've never seen a movie with both of them in it.

HA!

we both get misgendered by the waiter.

It's not a big deal for me, but B looks uncomfortable, and I think it hit a nerve.

I don't know why, but I always find it easier when a stranger does it.

Day Three: Today is the day of the show!

AFTER THE SHOW:

we stand right at the front and grab each others hands whenever they play a song we really like.

I can't believe how good that was.

Oh my god, I know! when they brought that kid onstage?

with B, I feel a sense of comfort I would not have expected to find this far from home.

I know our friendship will only grow from here.

A NOTE ON SAFETY: IF YOU DECIDE TO MEET UP WITH A NEW PERSON, MAKE SURE TO PRIORITIZE YOUR SAFETY, LET FRIENDS OR FAMILY KNOW WHERE YOU ARE AND HOW TO REACH YOU, AND HAVE A PLAN AND MONEY TO LEAVE IF NEED BE.

MEETING IN A PUBLIC PLACE IS ALWAYS BEST. I WAS A LEGAL ADULT WHEN I MET B, AND MADE SURE MY FRIENDS AND LOVED ONES KNEW WHERE I WAS AND HOW TO REACH ME, HAD CONTACT INFO FOR OUR HOTEL AND FOR B, TOO. I HAD A PLAN FOR LEAVING EARLY IF I NEEDED TO DO SO.

THE POWER IN QUESTIONING

The singer-songwriter on breaking out of self-doubt.

By Alessia Cara

"How do you learn to love yourself?"

It's a fair—and important!—question. And as a self-love advocate, I *want* to share some wise and life-changing revelation. Instead, I spent an awful lot of time staring at my computer screen, trying to come up with a profound way to say something that I . . . wait for it . . . honestly . . . hold on . . . don't have the answer to!

Hear me out. I can't create a guide to total self-confidence, because I haven't even completely guided myself to that goal yet. Yes, ladies and gentlemen. I'm Alessia, I'm 20 years old, I sing songs about self-love, and some days I don't like myself at all.

Sure, I've come a long way. I'm now very proud of who I am, and at the same time, very aware of who I'm not. But that doesn't mean I don't have to snap myself out of self-deprecation once in a while.

The reality is we all struggle, and unfortunately we often face unrealistic expectations over empowering ones. So we can receive compliments, read articles on self-esteem, or listen to a song by some girl who tells us we're beautiful a million times *cough*, and feel great. But the second we spot someone we wish we looked like, feel out of place amidst a group of people, or even stare at ourselves in the mirror for too long, it's tough not to stumble into a pit of self-consciousness and shame.

I've never understood this about us humans. Why does our awareness of the beautiful things fade so quickly, but the hurtful things stay painted on our psyches to torment us until we're back at square one? Another big question, and I don't have the answer to that either. But don't stop reading! I promise I'm getting somewhere.

Let's start here: The key is to ask questions. It's what leads us to our inner conclusions. In other words, being conscious that things don't make sense sometimes is the first step to making them make sense for you.

I'll give you an example.

All my life, when I would ask things like, "Why do people care about appearance so much?" or "Why does personality take a backseat to superficial standards?" I'd always get the same answer: "That's just the way it is."

My stubborn self wouldn't let that response be sufficient. Instead, I asked more questions, and I continue to ask them today.

"Who made these rules?"

"Why is that just the way it is?"

"How do my looks or others' expectations affect my capabilities?"

"Why should I listen?"

I have never and will never take "That's just the way it is" for an answer. Some may say that I question things just to question them or that I can't swallow the reality of being a young woman. But I find empowerment through my ability to question. The quicker I become aware that certain expectations lack reason, the quicker I realize they don't matter. I will keep asking these questions until I receive proper explanations, and the lack of answers proves what I already know: They don't exist, and never will.

The truth is that these impossible standards aren't real rules, but the ignorant views of closed-minded people. People's opinions of us reflect a microscopic aspect of who we are, and we are far more powerful and capable than they—and sometimes even we—can imagine. Now, I don't know if unconditional self-love is achievable. If it is, I'll admit that I'm not quite there yet. But I don't have to be. It's OK to feel insecure, and it's more than OK to doubt yourself at times. Believe it or not, it's part of human growth.

Knowing that the rules to "fitting in" aren't real is the first step to breaking them. Who says that ALL facets of my inner beauty can't be embraced? Why should I give in? How does my body define the woman/person I am? These are the things I constantly ask myself when I need a power boost, because, to me, the power to solve lives in the bravery to question.

So, lovely person reading this, the next time you feel yourself falling into that dark space again, answer your question with another.

Why should you love yourself?
Simple.
Why not?

ON LOVE AND ASSOCIATED LEAVINGS

You can't always keep people.

By Akwaeke Emezi

When I was 15 and studying at a private day school in Aba, Nigeria, my calculus instructor taught me to hoard myself. His name was Mr. Alpha and he was a strict but phenomenal teacher, the type it devastated me to disappoint. My best friend and I always sat in the front row of all his classes. We were inseparable—we'd been best friends my whole life, lived on the same street, rode to and from school together every day, since we were toddlers. One morning, she had to stay home and so I sat in the front alone, propping my chin on the desk. My attitude clouded around me—a sour metal gray, a loud resentment—dragging through the classroom air.

Halfway through the lesson, Mr. Alpha stopped midsentence to glare at me. "Is it because your friend is not here?" he said, exasperated.

I jerked in my seat and watched him walk over, certain I was going to get scolded in front of everybody. But instead, as Mr. Alpha got closer and looked at my face, his own softened with unexpected kindness.

"You can never give one hundred percent of yourself to someone," he said, keeping his voice at the same volume so that everyone in the class could hear and learn. "It's not good. If they leave, then what happens to you?"

It's been another 15 years since that classroom and I still think, *What a good question.* What *does* happen to you when they leave? Do you walk around unwhole, with an empty space knocking about inside you, echoing so loudly you wonder how other people can't hear it? Do you fill it with louder things, like tequila or wine or weed or a stranger's arm thrown across your belly? Or maybe you're like me—you wall it off and pretend that the space was never full, that it doesn't even exist anymore. When I left my best friend to go to college in America, I decided that I was going to put all of my energy into avoiding loss. It was too brutal; it made too little sense. I was 16, and somehow, I ended up believing that the only safety against being left was for someone to love you so hard that they *couldn't* leave, so hard that the very act of losing you would devastate them, render them nonfunctional and broken. You would be safe with them precisely because their only safety would be in staying with you. Looking back now, it seems like more of a hostage situation, but this, I thought, was love.

After college, I got married to a man who believed his ideal life was only possible with me: I was the key, the gateway, the escape. In the realm of proof, he'd already left another life for the one he could see with me. We were in New York and I'd just turned 22. When we ended, as I left and watched him shatter, my certainty that he loved me remained unshaken. I was devastated, yes, but I was functional—Mr. Alpha had taught me well. I'd become guarded with giving but greedy with taking; obsessed with being loved but unconcerned with learning how to love anyone else properly. Instead, I offered intensity, passion— I burned up the air around me and cloaked my intentions in a glamour that distracted people.

As the divorce was processing, I was dating a girl who tried to break up with me at the restaurant where I worked. On that day, as soon as my shift ended, I went to her apartment and played ABBA's "Take a Chance on Me" out of my phone's speaker. I wanted to keep her, even though I wasn't going to give her what she wanted. I didn't care. She wasn't allowed to leave me. I smiled with relief when she called me corny, because I knew it meant she was staying. When I was ready, I left her and fell in love with another girl, and when this one tried to leave me, after our fights and her hands around my neck and my glass of orange juice missing her head and shattering against the wall and the screaming and the crying and the locked bathroom door, I cut myself to make her stay. No one leaves me.

The next person I fell in love with was someone else's husband and father. I threw myself out of a chair at his house, screaming and crying because he had threatened to leave me, my body convulsing at his feet. He watched, satisfied. If you have a cruel streak, there is pleasure in knowing someone loves you more than you love them. It makes you feel powerful. In your mind, they shift. Their smell changes. It becomes soft, weak. They become a thing you can hunt or disregard or pounce on or bend just for the fun of seeing how long they take to break.

At my apartment, he walked into my tiny bathroom as I stood at the sink. "You're sick," he said, but gently, because he wanted me to believe it, too. "There's something wrong with you." Then, his voice over a phone as I sobbed and hyperventilated. "Go and kill yourself." And still, me weeping on the floor of his house, begging not to lose him. No one leaves me. Months later, when I left him, he punched the dashboard of his truck, over and over as we drove toward my place, his infant son lying in the car seat next to me. I watched, satisfied.

Sometimes, I couldn't tell the difference between how I felt and what I wanted people to believe I was feeling, because lies work best if you believe them, too. I tried to make myself into everything they could ever want, just so they could need me: a customized dream, a specific snare. I met men who mistook that for malleability and it made them comfortable. They felt I would never leave, that I needed them; that the love I held for them made me weak, a sure and spineless thing. It's a common mistake—thinking that just because someone doesn't want you to leave them, they're not preparing to leave you.

We leverage love in such predictable ways, trying to keep people with it, wanting suffering as proof. If someone can leave you without being destroyed, you think their love wasn't true. It seems impossible that someone could love you and yet, walk away. You're supposed to stay. You're not supposed to be able to live without the other person. Even within friendships, to abandon someone you love reads as a hostile act. You're supposed to make it work.

I've done that—spent hours trying to fix things, waited weeks for a friend I fell in love with to care that our everything was in jeopardy, defended my humanity to a loved one who wouldn't see their privilege—but sometimes, you realize that the thing you're trying to change is the other person, and that's when, love or not, you should probably stop. In that moment, take stock. You can accept this thing about them, this thing they've said or done that they have no remorse for, or you can refuse, and leave. Some people choose to stay, fighting to make the other person see what's wrong, so they can care enough to fix it. I don't believe in that, mostly because I won't fight for the validity of my pain to be recognized by someone who's supposed to care about me. Not anymore. Nowadays, I just leave. An old and familiar choice, yes, but it looks different this time. It moves and feels and tastes like something else.

Before, when I was younger and unleashed, I left people either because I was selfish and I'd kept them longer than I should have, or because they treated me terribly and my leaving was timed retaliation. But then years passed and the losses kept coming, whether I planned them or not, and the emptiness knocked about inside me, and I got tired. It stopped mattering if people left because, I realized, everything is susceptible to an ending. You can't control it. You can bend yourself into unthought-of contortions, you can flail and cry and beg, you can love so hard that you reek of desperation, and it does nothing. It does nothing. Rejection still happens, and after a while, even manipulating people feels pointless. I had always been the perpetrator or the victim or, sometimes, marvelously, both, and I was tired. I found myself wanting love where I was safe, where no one had to suffer because everyone was always tender, always careful, where hurts were accidental and not malicious, where we (lovers or friends) were soft with one another because, to be quite honest, the rest of the world is wicked enough for all our lifetimes.

When the loves I have fall short of these criteria, I leave. It hurts, yes, but I don't want a love that makes me miserable. Not anymore. So I leave people I love, even if it makes me the villain in their story—the one who fucked up and failed, who threw away the friendship without giving it a chance, who didn't care. Our criteria for love are wildly subjective. Sometimes, I want to talk to people I left and reassure them that I didn't leave with anger, that if I was really being a villain, I would do it well and without remorse, as I have before—I would never need to hide it. I liked it too much. But also that this is not the same, this time I didn't want to leave, but I had to, that I'm not sorry, that I love them, I love them, I still love them.

I haven't been back to that classroom in Aba since my graduation, but I can still see Mr. Alpha standing there in khaki trousers, his face pulled into a knowing smile. I can still feel his lesson set inside my chest. It's all grown up now, just like me, and it reminds me that I can't control anyone else or their story. I am the only person who belongs to me. No one else does. You can leave me. You can stay. You belong to yourself. What love means, after all, is that every single day, you get to choose.

ASTAGHFIRULLAH*: A KISS BEFORE DYING

By Bassey Ikpi

you render me useless this side of morning
more than the weight of left leg
draped heavily against right
more than muscled shoulders
tattooed with sweat
and last night's perfume
or locks wrapped around fist
pinned against sheets
cooling from wet

i want to struggle and roll into the part of this
i own
but my last lover was so slight of a man
that he crushed my lungs with his indifference
i still haven't learned to exhale properly

you are thick bundles of muted air

and when the silence and shadows
hit your face
more like him than i care to be responsible for

* I beg Allah for forgiveness.

still, i welcome your weight
the obscene arrogance of your manhood
bass and jazz song voice

we laugh about grown folks business
avoid the truth so often
we forget it exists
astaghfirullah

i welcome you a trapped,
unfinished verse
read on borrowed time

delicate balance of secrets and trumpets
i long to stretch angle cut of glass
and cheek
brass and bone
burn me stubble of stubborn promised beard
twisted plum lips
inviting
this regrettable love song

this brooklyn impossible
this wrong side of the tracks affair
this pebbled stone and grit
this wish that you
would wake under the swollen pull
that begs for you

let me whisper this wish into the last star before morning:
kiss me like we are dying
like time travelers seeking home
beneath tangled tongues and clicking teeth

no, kiss me like i'm dying
allow me to feed on the flesh of this bottom lip
you, ripe fruit of a mouth

take hold this treaty between
breath and heartbeat
the war is in the longing
the
quiet
let's not sully this with questions
of fidelity
or love

own it flat
peppered
crust and mortar
lust and anger
fuck me like an inappropriate love song
naked with the ghost of your rejected youth
the first encouraged broken shards of heart
the second fed it to her next lover
while you watched
the last bore you a mirror
that reflects your father
you love her so much; it smells like a well-crafted hatred
and i'm here
struggling against the nothing we created
twice already
twice more before the sun returns home
before i return home

so for just a moment, the clock on the window
will read 4:58,

the sky will split open
spilling morning onto this sacred city block
whisper
5:00 is when it must end
roll back and search for last night in the still dark of bedroom
allow your weight to shift
freeing the serpentine locks from the prison of the last hour

invite the weight
return to the quiver at the end of fingertips
serving one more sacred sacrifice
a salah into the morning
one more honest prayer before god wakes
an offering
an understanding
something like
one more hallowed and
careful hallelujah
before the sun

Astaghfirullah

LONESOME COWBOY

Finding dimension in quiet gestures.

By Hilton Als

The thing seemingly freely given often isn't. It is rare to receive the gift of love, for instance, from someone who doesn't want to be celebrated for their generosity in having offered it; altruism is often a dream. But there are those who connect through the truth of love—the irrefutable force of it—establishing a mutual bond grounded in reality and not the theater of the giver's "I." It's odd, but wouldn't you say that in our universe of worked-out bodies and worked-out minds, that to be receptive is looked upon as "weak," a passive vessel for someone else's love and dreams? So, instead of embracing the generosity inherent in being able to accept love, the receptors among us punish themselves by adopting stereotypical "needy" behavior, warping their instincts to look "active," the better to satisfy an audience's view of what it means to be open. Rather than saying, *Oh! I miss you! Give me* you *for however long you can*, the receptor playing to the audience says: *You must see me now!* Which has the opposite desired effect, of course.

How can we reverse the negativity that surrounds being receptive—to love, to someone else's dreams? What are we supposed to do with this space? Stare down into it? Put flowers in it? Shout out to the less receptive among us that there is nothing wrong with *saying* what one wants, including love? I don't know. Just don't call me until you're ready to receive, and I'm ready to give. One sees flowers growing around Montgomery Clift's mouth at the end of that black-and-white masterpiece, *A Place in the Sun* (1951). The flowers grow in the earth of his receptivity—his openness to the scene, the atmosphere. In all aspects of his work Clift was, to my mind and eye, the greatest film actor this country has ever produced, largely because he jettisoned acting out for acting in. He embodied receptivity. While others feel that Marlon Brando was the Greatest Ever, Clift didn't rely on what Brando never left behind: the conventional stage, and the predictable mechanics of theatricalization. But Brando was smart enough about the human psyche to understand that it thrives on the known, and that "sexiness" depends on declaring itself outright: Audiences don't want to dig for it since they spend so much time at home, digging for their own. Brando was a master showman who was perfectly well aware, too, that the actor—the walking figment of one's imagination—increases his power over an audience if he can convince them of this imagined fact: He'll break the fourth wall (or screen) and claim them. And isn't that what everyone wants, ultimately—to be claimed? Clift, a much more recessive personality and controlled screen artist, couldn't find himself in bombast, and it was his constant reducing during a scene— hand gestures that quieted down, and then stopped; a slight jerking of his small frame when Marilyn Monroe extends her compassion in a bottle-strewn junkyard in 1961's literally and figuratively fantastic *The Misfits*—that was essential to his screen presence as well, that white flat movie-place Clift filled with one character again and again: the unknown but often despised one. (This character reached his apex when Clift played Freud in John Huston's 1962 biopic, or shall we say bio-poem?

Original script? By Sartre!) Clift's poetry was in the drama of emotional mishap: characters who didn't like his character because he was a Jew, or a murderer, or Something Else. As such, he upstaged Hitchcock's fabled love of cinema minimalism when he played a priest in the director's strange 1953 film, *I Confess*. Clift's utterly compelling under-the-emotional-radar-but-with-heart-and-guilt-cutting-his-breath-short-at-nearly-every-turn show underscores that, while Hitchcock hated "acting," he didn't know what to do when an actor was even better at being a "model" than his rage and manipulation could demand. And since that tension doesn't exist for Hitch with Clift, the movie is without tension.

Another story about the modernist-minded performer: In 1961 he was making *Judgment at Nuremberg*, with Stanley Kramer. Judy Garland was in the film. Kramer invited Clift to watch a take featuring Judy, and when Kramer turned to Clift after the take was over, tears were streaming down Clift's cheeks. Kramer: "Ah, wasn't Judy marvelous?" Clift, crying: "No." Because she's playing her character's tragedy even before she opens her mouth. While beautiful, Clift was rarely considered "sexy," because he couldn't even claim himself; his effects depended on you going in and finding his unspoken pain or joy—the erotics of silence—behind his pale skin, dark hair, and character-defining posture. (A sensitive straight male acquaintance, explaining Clift to his girlfriend, who had never seen him in a film, said: "Listen, I'm not into men, at all, but with him. Wow.") While Brando played cowboys, Clift was the quintessential lonesome cowboy, a tumbleweed of reduced-for-the-camera everything: desperation, loneliness, hope. While it's almost impossible to remember what Clift said in a movie, or how he said it, you can remember what Brando said because, despite his fabled laxness with the script, what he said was scripted; he was enough of a stage actor to believe it began with the playwright or screenwriter, while Clift's modernism had little to do with language and everything to do with being watched, and letting the surrounding air be the improvisation. In silent-film terms, Brando was Chaplin, and Clift, Keaton. Watching Montgomery Clift taught me that there is no shame in being receptive to a given situation or person; it is part of my job as an artist, and part of who I am as a man in search of love and its flowers.

PAST EXPOSURE

The look of love.

By Collier Meyerson

There's an old black-and-white photo of the 20th-century feminist writer and thinker Simone de Beauvoir doing her hair in a Chicago bathroom. She's around 40. Her ass is plump; a few sexy dimples ride down the back of her upper right thigh. Her left leg stands sturdily out in front, and she's leaning a bit on her right hip. All she's got on are a pair of heels. It's easy to imagine this was how de Beauvoir always did her hair, no matter who was watching. But it also seems she liked it when someone *did* watch.

I know the photo was taken during her affair with the writer Nelson Algren. It's always struck me as a lover's photo, sexily surreptitious, the kind of candid snapped in a moment of pure ecstatic longing, when your lover is doing something terribly normal, their hair, and it takes your breath away. This photo guarantees Algren's love—because no one can take a photo like this and not be.

And I know from reading de Beauvoir's love letters to Algren that their relationship didn't last. It's the kind of picture you find in a drawer beneath a bunch of other shit a while after you've ended a relationship, tears involuntarily collecting in your eyes and vomit in your throat. A photo you study, wishing for the time before that massive love was corrupted.

I first saw the photograph on Tumblr, years ago, and assumed Algren took it. In fact, it was a photographer and friend of Algren's,

Art Shay. The photo wasn't the deeply erotic and intimate portrait of a woman by the man who loves her, but, instead, the deeply erotic portrait of a woman performing intimacy. Equally as heated, but different. For show, for others' consumption. Like Instagram.

I have some photos like the one of Simone de Beauvoir. Physical pictures of a boyfriend during the first half of my 20s. In one, he's sitting shirtless on our balcony in Chicago looking at me, his mouth slightly agape as if he were about to whisper, "I love you." My memory is that's exactly what he said: "I love you, Collier." I keep them all in a blue folder with old love letters and other loose photos from my past, memories that feel inappropriate to collect in a photo album but impossible to throw away.

Lovers' photos were often private then. Unless, of course, they were art, made to be consumed, like the one of de Beauvoir.

And then culture shifted. In my next serious relationship, I didn't use a Polaroid or disposable camera. Instead, I started to snap my most intimate romantic moments on Instagram. All of the photos I took of my next boyfriend—I'll call him Eli—were impulsive, a frivolous record of intimacy I rarely revisited because I never imagined the relationship would end. But it did. And there's no blue folder to keep him in.

I wasn't an artist, like Shay. But I was inducted into a new phenomenon with old roots: performing my love.

In the first few weeks we started dating, Eli sent flowers to my job, and desserts over to the table at a restaurant he knew I was at with friends. Since we were long distance, we spent hours on FaceTime in those first months. Once or twice we fell asleep still on the phone at dawn. He texted me article links demanding my opinion, and he'd call me on the phone to excoriate anyone who disagreed with something I'd written or said. As an outspoken critic of Israel, I'd call him at least once a week incensed at the country's latest act of provocation against Palestinians. He called me the most beautiful woman he'd ever seen; sometimes, he'd say it ten times a day. And I responded by texting him a blurry picture of every funny bumper sticker I saw on the road, because he loved silly bumper stickers. I'd never been swept off my feet quite like it; he was intoxicating. I was all he thought about. I could be myself, and he worshipped me—a first.

I wanted my universe to know I loved. But something else, too, nagged at me: I wanted the universe to know I *was* loved.

The first photo I took of Eli was on one of his first visits. He had a boyish aversion to greens. The photo is a split screen: a before and after of him eating the eggs and kale I'd made for us. I remember how tickled I was by his true, uncontrolled laugh.

A couple of months later, we went on a road trip through California, and he documented the whole thing on Instagram. "Smitten," said the one he took on the beach after we'd run for our lives to catch the sunset. I look out of breath and my hair was wild from the wind, but it's one of those unmistakable lover's photos: I wasn't even thinking about the camera, all I cared about was what was just beyond it.

Whenever I looked at engagement and wedding photos on Facebook, I thought that they felt different from Instagram photos. Professional photos were put-on, I thought, staged love to show the grandkids. The Instagram photos I took of Eli felt more intimate, something the grandkids would swipe through one night when I restored the clunky old app after reminiscing about how we used to revolve our lives around it.

But on second thought, my Instagram photos weren't so different in their purpose. They, too, were expressions to my universe that I was desired. Trips, meals, weddings, quiet nights at home, were all punctuated by Eli's love for me. And that was real, that was my life, and if Instagram is a curated documentation of both the mundane and the celebratory moments of life, then that was a true reflection. But I also had the feeling that showing the world I was in love gave me a sense of purpose I hadn't had while I was single. The mounting "likes" made me, a woman who isn't generally interested in being defined by men, feel more affirmed.

At 4 AM, a year and three months after Eli and I broke up, I opened Instagram and began scrolling through all the photos of us when we were together. I began looking at the photos tagged of him, ones I took of him, and ones someone else took of us. I began to cry at the one I posted of us under a giant waterfall in upstate New York. I wore a crimson vintage one-piece and Eli was naked. I had used an app to cover his dick and my caption read, "He's so shy, that sweet little boy who caught my eye." That weekend away was the first trip we took with my friends. I had been nervous that they wouldn't like one another, but they did, and I fell more in love with him for it.

After I'd looked at all the photos tagged of him, I moved on to the photos tagged of me. I liked the one our friend Jacob took of us: Eli, in his shiny satin Celtics jacket, crouched over me, biting my neck. Underneath him, I was laughing, my half-hot PBR like a prop to my right.

It had been a month since I stopped responding to Eli's texts and phone calls. I unfollowed him on Instagram after he posted a photo with his new girlfriend. I told myself I'd stop looking at him altogether on Instagram. Now that he had a girlfriend, I didn't need to obsessively check his new followers, to see which new women he was following, or who might be commenting on his photos. I didn't need to wonder. But, I was awake at 4 AM, and already in despair. I wanted more agony, so much more—my heart an unstoppable, grotesque, malevolent monster.

By 5 AM, I was studying the photos I'd posted of myself since becoming single. Sometimes I look happy, like when I was singing along to Rihanna, arms raised, in Zoila's convertible in Joshua Tree. But weren't a lot of them also performances of happiness, too? Instagram is a hellscape.

I deleted the app and cried until the sun came up, and then I closed my eyes and fell asleep.

A GUIDE TO FALLING IN LOVE, TELESERYE STYLE

Fate! Mystery! Mishap! Romance!

By Gaby Gloria

Real love is two people looking into each other's eyes, complete with sparkles, chiming sound effects, a killer instrumental, and earnest background narration along the lines of "They say that when you fall in love, time will stop. You'll hear the loud thumping of your heart. I never thought it would happen to me."

As a college senior whose relationship status is currently NBSB (no boyfriend since birth), I tend to think big when it comes to romance. And as I'm coming from the Philippines, with a culture that's basically in love with the idea of love, it's hard not to.

Filipinos are *obsessed* with romance, and they aren't ashamed to show it. The Filipino language even has a word for that cute butterflies-in-your-tummy fluttering sensation that you get when you're in love: kilig. The word is so rooted in Filipino culture that English has no equivalent.

The thing about kilig is that it can come in secondary forms. You can say, "Nakikilig ako" (I'm feeling kilig), while listening to a friend give you the juicy details of her first date, or while watching the main characters of your fave film finally kiss.

Every year, the Filipino film industry capitalizes on kilig by churning out rom-com after rom-com starring local celebrities, who are often paired up in multiple film and TV projects—a partnership that's literally called a "love team." People in the Philippines often spend their weeknights parked in front of their TVs to see if the leads finally get together in their favorite teleserye, a soap opera that runs for a couple of months.

Most of the time, these shows are centered on the idea of destiny. The narratives are ultimately pretty cheesy: the main characters are tied together by a literal red string of fate, or a loud heartbeat is the best indicator you're with your true love. Teleseryes go heavy on the melodrama, rehashing versions of the same story with tropes you can also find in Korean dramas, Spanish telenovelas, and Japanese shojo manga.

I've been through my fair share of crushes and getting crushed, but none of them have ever escalated to the point of a romantic relationship. I don't know what it's like for a boy to ask me out or even to tell me that he likes me. But thanks to all the things I've watched, I have other expectations of how these things *should* go. Immersing myself in these concepts poses the risk of viewing the world with a teleserye-tinted filter.

Let's be real: Finding and sustaining a real-life relationship seems exhausting. If we lived our lives following predictable plot points, things would be so much easier. At least in teleseryes, all the bida (protagonist) has to do is live his or her life to be guaranteed a happy ending.

But what if I told you that you can be the bida of your very own life teleserye? That you have a formula you can follow to meet The One? You're in luck, for I mapped out some common plot points to get you started. Follow these guidelines, and you'll be cruising on the road to true love in no time!

1. SET YOUR SIGHTS ON YOUR SIGNIFICANT OTHER-TO-BE

It could be anyone, but keep your eyes open for specific archetypes, especially those who seem like arrogant richies.

Did you accidentally make eye contact with the brooding guy in the wide-rimmed glasses from your philosophy class? Do you fancy the eccentric girl playing the ukulele at lunch? Or has a handsome Prince Charming saved you from tripping over your own feet? No need to think this through—they're definitely your soulmate.

2. DEVISE A MEET CUTE

Like in typical rom-coms, the meet cute is an essential part of any teleserye. It usually happens by way of literally bumping into them on a busy street, but a couple of variations exist: You might meet after a thief nabs something from your pockets in a busy palengke (public market). Or maybe a person happens to be parachuting down a mountain just as you're driving your strawberry truck along said mountain (like in *Forevermore*). Just make sure that you come off as the love interest in distress. It's also important to note that you've already met as children, but, of course, neither of you remembers.

3. MAKE SURE THAT YOU GET OFF ON THE WRONG FOOT

Even if you already know that you're destined to fall in love with your person, you've got to play hard to get. Make the other person hate you first to build up that sexual tension by doing things to annoy them. Try screaming at your love dove or "accidentally" spilling your drink on their shirt.

4. FIND A CONVENIENT CIRCUMSTANCE THAT WILL FORCE YOU TO BOND

Engineer an opportunity to get way closer, whether you get yourself paired up on a class project or got "creative" with your résumé to land a job at their company. It'll look like fate has brought you together!

5. GET AN OUTSIDE FORCE TO THREATEN YOUR BUDDING RELATIONSHIP

From the low-stakes, out-of-place emotional outburst and drunk confession or the entrance of a third party to the more extreme car crash + amnesia/hospital arc or warehouse kidnapping, these plot devices only serve to shake everything up and provide more opportunities for you two to get even closer. Don't worry, your undying love for each other will cause the conflict to automatically fix itself, when the kontrabida (antagonist) undoes all the mistakes they made.

6. SIT BACK, RELAX, AND ENJOY THE RIDE

Now all you've got to do is chill out and prepare for your happily ever after. Heads up: It's probably going to be a church wedding, complete with a hundred of your closest friends (including a bunch of minor characters and very distant cousins) in attendance.

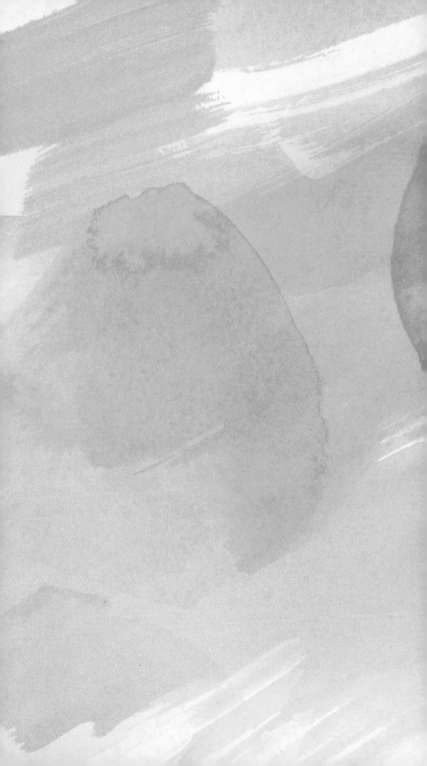

RADIANCE

On being a creature of light.

By Maria Popova

One unusually chilly September, I found myself in the middle of southern nowhere, on a midwifery farm founded in the 1970s and practically unchanged since. My dear friend Amanda— a born-and-raised New Englander who had rebelled by becoming an artist and growing a large hippie heart—had journeyed there to give birth.

There was an eerie and exhilarating time-travel feeling to the farm—secluded and rudimentary, it was a freeze-frame of civilization taken in a different era. When night fell, it fell completely. Darkness engulfed the land—the kind of darkness those of us nursed on urban over-illumination have forgotten exists, darkness punctuated only by glimmers of celestial light poking through the thinning autumn foliage.

One starless night, Amanda and I ventured out of the cabin for an after-dinner walk. We didn't take a flashlight, or even a phone. We had walked the single road backboning the farm many times in the daylight, so we decided to revere the darkness and trust our creaturely spatial instincts. Unable to see more than five feet ahead, we discerned the general direction of the road from the clearing above the trees, where the cloudy nocturne seemed slightly less dark than the heavy darkness surrounding us—darkness so thick that each stride seemed to slice the air apart. We walked slowly yet assuredly, arm in arm. Strapped to

Amanda's chest was her newborn son. Strapped to mine, the heartache of a longtime relationship that had just ended.

Right as we were about to revolve back toward the house, a most extraordinary sight arrested us: in the middle of the woods, a meadowy clearing revealed itself, sprinkled with what appeared to be a galaxy of fallen stars. Hundreds, perhaps thousands of them, whose lights flickered gently in slow motion. I gasped at the marvel, the unanticipated beauty. It took me a moment and some deeply buried vestige of ninth-grade biology to realize they were glowworms—piercing the darkness like a living constellation, a masterwork of nature perfected through millennia of meticulous evolution. And the most remarkable thing, the most poetic thing, was that they didn't glow to delight us onlookers—they glowed to find one another in the dark.

I often think of the glowworms, of how every love song ever written, every romantic poem and play and movie, is but the luminescent halo of this elemental longing to reach across the darkness of being and find another creature with whom to share this life. "We crave radiance in this austere world," wrote the poet Elizabeth Alexander ("Allegiance," *Crave Radiance*, 2010), and crave it we do, though perhaps less obviously and more self-consciously than these tiny earthen insects. And I don't know whether Daniel Johnston was right to sing, the year I was born, that "true love will find you in the end" ("True Love Will Find You in the End," *Retired Boxer,* 1985). But I do know that it helps to give off a little light—to never cease being a creature of radiance, even in your darkest hour.

210

UNDER PRESSURE

Your terms, your timeline.

By Victoria Chiu

I'm not really one for sappiness, but I'm totally, completely, unabashedly in love. I'm in love after many years of thinking I would never experience this kind of love, and I'm thankful that for the last two and a half years, I've been fortunate to have someone who understands me; who hugs and kisses me when I need comforting; and who, above all, makes me feel super, super special—like I'm a shining, priceless jewel when I feel like dull, dusty coal.

People in my life, when they find out I've been dating my person, E, this long now, often ask, "How far have you two gone?" They mean sexually, of course. And while it's uncomfortable to answer under most circumstances—at least for me—it becomes even more awkward when the well-intentioned friend offers up their own guess. Almost every time, they assume E and I have already breached that "final frontier"—that we've had some sort of genital-to-genital or penetrative sex—simply because of how long we've been together. When I debunk this assumption, they're shocked or surprised: For a lot of people my age (19) or older, the near-automatic expectation is that people who date exclusively will sleep together within a year (if not much sooner), and those who go beyond that are outliers.

We had our first kiss after close to two months of dating. The timing felt just right to me, but many of our friends said otherwise.

"That's a reeeeeally long wait," our friend Q commented gingerly. He'd kissed his then-girlfriend the same day they'd begun dating, and they'd made their way around the proverbial bases within six months. Other friends, O and J, had gone even faster. It was a bit unusual to wait longer, they said, because there wasn't really a reason to. If you liked that person, weren't opposed to sex on principle, and didn't face any barriers to being together, why wouldn't you dive into the physical side of a relationship?

I couldn't articulate an answer then, but I knew somewhere deep within me that sex, penetrative sex, wasn't quite right for me. Not yet. It still isn't. All this talk about how quickly everyone else seemed to move made me feel as if I were running behind on some invisible schedule—though nobody told me that I *should* have sex, or that I was somehow sexually off course, I felt the pressure of an intangible force. I felt it whenever I saw high schoolers getting busy after dating a few weeks in movies, and I sensed it when I read accounts of guys who couldn't wait to "score" after three dates. I was never confronted with it outright, but it cloaked me in its weight when I allowed my mind to wander. There was no escape.

Another "shocker": E and I haven't taken a vow of celibacy. We aren't against premarital sex (far from it), and we aren't put off by sex, either. The choice to not have penetrative sex was made largely on my part, but it's just that: a choice, an expression of personal preference. And for the most part, people respect that—everyone has their own stance on sex. But occasionally, someone will interpret our present abstinence as prudishness.

One night, E was on Skype playing *League of Legends* with a friend, P, when the topic of sex came up. P, after finding out our sexual history, reacted immediately with something akin to revulsion.

"Dude, what are you *doing*? Are you, like, waiting for marriage or some shit?"

We aren't, and E said so, which led to even more confusion. Why, then, P wondered aloud, wouldn't we just jump in and fucking do it already? Wasn't it weird to be dating for so long without having sex? This wasn't the Victorian era.

To put it simply, it's complicated. Although a vow of celibacy might give other people an explanation for our "holding out," the honest truth is that it's a combination of factors. Here are the facts:

I. A ROMANTIC RELATIONSHIP
WITHOUT SEX ≠ "JUST FRIENDSHIP"

Penetrative sex—any sex, in fact—isn't some sort of magical hallmark that validates a romantic relationship. Being in love doesn't inherently imply having sex, even if our society places so much emphasis on penetrative—and particularly P-in-V—sex. It comes up in movies and songs, and it's used on billboards and TV to sell everything from perfume to handbags. Given how frequently we're bombarded with it, it's no wonder our society is so sex-obsessed—so much so that lack of sex, the lack of primal lust and desire, tends to signal (to some people) "friends-only." But sex isn't a barometer of intimacy, which is something I personally associate with love. And lust, based on sexual spark, can often quickly fade. So if a relationship doesn't involve sexual acts, it doesn't mean it's somehow less full, less rich, less gratifying and passionate.

Any romantic relationship between people of any gender can be fulfilling and passionate with or without sex in its varying degrees. And anyone continuing to push the "sex = real relationship" narrative is, frankly, more than a little wrong.

II. WAITING TO HAVE SEX ≠
BEING "UNFAIR" TO YOUR PARTNER

Some people think that one partner's unwillingness to have sex is unfair to the other person—another point P brought up that game night. That was something that bothered me for a long time, especially since my partner has a very high sex drive. I do too (that isn't one of the reasons why I'm waiting). But because of the remarks of some individuals in my life and constant messages from mainstream media, I thought that I wasn't doing my "duty" as a partner if I wasn't willing to do this tale-as-old-as-time sex thing. It gave me a lot of anxiety, because I care so much about E and I would never want to do anything that would be unfair to him.

I spent many weeks turning over P's words in my mind, torturing myself over the negative impact I must be having on E, and worrying about how he felt about me as a result. But once I whispered my fears to him one night over the phone, I found that they were unfounded. E was actually a little insulted I would think that he would take that kind of attitude toward sex. Sex is a two-party deal, he reminded me, and there was no way any relationship could function if one person was prioritizing their own needs so highly, without considering the feelings of the other. He loved me, he said, and because of that, any sex would only be enjoyable if I liked it and was comfortable with it, too.

Not to be cheesy, but I felt my heart swell when I heard that. Maybe it was love, because of his feelings for me, or maybe it was relief that he understood how I felt. It was probably both.

III. NOT GOING "ALL THE WAY" ≠ ZERO SEX LIFE

My guess as to why "we haven't gone all the way" is often met with such bewilderment is that the people who hear it take it to mean E and I have no sex life. That's not true. We've done other things in the ballpark (we've been "around the bases," if you will), and we indulge in them pretty frequently, but we haven't done that final act. For some people, that somehow isn't enough. To them, if you're not engaging in one very specific form of sex, you're not really having sex at all.

To put it clearly, if you want to have sex, there's no one correct "way" of doing it. Consensual sex in a relationship is a lovely, beautiful thing. It's a way to express love, but it isn't the only way. I want to fit in and to feel like I'm "on schedule" with everyone else around me, and yet I don't feel ready for it at 19. I try to remember, when I feel doubtful and freakish, that all of my feelings are normal and valid. It's OK to want to have sex, and it's OK not to. Everything comes in time, it's said, and I think my confusing, sometimes conflicting feelings on this, too, will crystallize in the future.

One day I will want to have (penetrative) sex. I've been warming to the idea recently. I don't know when it will happen, or how, but I do feel that it *will* happen. One day. When it does, I'll feel comfortable and enthusiastic about it. It'll be a non-decision, because I'll know through my whole being that I want it. Until that day, I'll focus on what I have right now, and how fantastic it already is. The late-night phone calls, the cuddles, the makeout sessions, and the countless hours of company and understanding and love, love, *love*. Love that fills my soul and surrounds me. I can figure out the sex stuff later. After all, it's no rush.

FRIENDS FOR LIFE

Find yourself a circle where you can be your most human.

By Diamond Sharp

I've fallen in love with friends in the back of cabs, over dinner, and in the ephemeral confines of social-media DMs. The women I've connected with are the ones who ground me when life goes left and lift me up when everything is going swimmingly. Since entering my 20s, I've thought a lot about the type of friendships I want—it's still a radical position to think of your platonic friendships as of equal importance to your romantic relationships. But these purposeful friendships I've crafted have been the backbone of my growth.

To me, a purposeful friendship is a relationship with another person who can *see* you. Purposeful friends accept you for who you are, even when you're not your best self. These people are invested in you for the long haul. Reciprocity is a given—when I think of my closest friendships, I see women with whom I feel restored after getting together. Friendship doesn't prevent life from going awry, but it provides folks you can fall back on. But at their best, my deliberate friendships are sustaining, and I've fallen in love with my friends unapologetically.

My friendships weren't always like this. Friendship is weird because you're essentially telling a stranger, "Hello! I like you and would like to keep you around forever. Cool?" Just like in a romantic relationship, it's possible you may kiss a few proverbial frogs while figuring out who fulfills you. In high school, I took cues from shows like *Girlfriends* and *A Different World* reruns: I wanted a circle that was unbreakable. I tried on and dropped friends; our connections were largely superficial (maybe because I was trying to model my friendships on fictional portrayals). It wasn't until college that I made lasting friends. It's cliché to talk about the bond students form at a women's school, but it was a true phenomenon for me. My time at Wellesley taught me to be unafraid of intimate friendships with women. Now that I'm firmly planted in my adult life, I've built my relationships on a mutual interest to be unafraid of love in friendship.

To be black and a woman means existing at an intersection of being unseen and objectified. Within the coterie of black women I surround myself with, I am *seen*—I am allowed to be my most human. With them, I can sit in silence or be loud, cry, or be a complete mess. I'm able to be a complex person among the black women I've forged bonds with in a way that I cannot be to the world writ large.

And yet, sometimes, it feels like friendships are discounted or treated as substitutes. There is a saying that blood is thicker than water—meaning that your biological family will always stand by you in a way you can't trust your friends to do. I also live in a country where it is expected that your partner or spouse can be your everything. Perhaps that is true for some, but I never want it to be my reality that my friendships have fallen to the wayside. My early 20s coincided with my onset of bipolar II disorder—I've spent a lot of time getting back to who I was before the illness. When I think about my darkest moments, I remember the friends who let me sleep over the nights my hypomania became too much for me to handle on my own. Or the friend who helped me pack for my first hospitalization. Or the friend who attempted to sneak a cupcake past hospital security because she wanted to cheer me up. My lowest lows have not been the end of me, in no small part because of the community of women I'm a part of.

I've been lucky to have friends who see me completely and know when things are wrong, even if I'm not yet aware. All of these women have taught me to be my best self. I'm unafraid to tell my friends that I love them and mean it.

In her novel *Beloved*, Toni Morrison wrote, "She is a friend of my mind. She gather me, man. The pieces I am, she gather them and give them back to me in all the right order." That is the beauty of the friendships I have. I am able to be both unfinished and complete, knowing that my friends will be present whether I'm in pieces or whole.

INFINITE LOVE

Does first mean forever?
By Upasna Barath

When I was younger, the only thing I knew about love was it had an end. Love—romantic love—had stops. My mother married, remarried, and remarried again. As I watched her struggle in her relationships, true love, the kind in the books I devoured, felt foreign to me. And yet, my mother took that third chance. And despite my uncertainty about what being in love really meant, I wanted to have faith that I would experience it, too.

As a kid, I constantly daydreamed about my nonexistent relationship: how my future boyfriend and I would meet, what we'd say, our first kiss. My go-to fantasy was inspired by one of my favorite movies at the time, *The Princess Diaries*. I loved the relationship that blossomed between Mia Thermopolis (average teen, surprise royal) and her best friend's brother, Michael (hot keyboardist, hardworking mechanic). I'd play out a personalized version in my head: older (cooler) me, spending time with a boy I secretly liked and who secretly liked me back, both of us basking in the tension that existed due to our inability to tell each other how we felt. I didn't have any real-life evidence of how people actually met and fell in love, but: being myself, crushing on someone, failing to communicate—and having it lead to a "foot-popping kiss" like Mia's and happily ever after? I could do that. It seemed that simple.

My mother's first two marriages were painful and ended badly. Witnessing her hurt, bewildered by and angry at the actions of my father and stepfather made me desperate for reassurance that love existed and could really happen for me. So I searched for models of romance in the books I read. One way I could fall in love: among action and adventure, falling deep for my best friend, as Ron and Hermione do in the Harry Potter series. Or through an awkward and thrilling kiss even in the middle of dealing with difficult family issues (I could really relate), like in Sharon Creech's novel *Walk Two Moons*. Sure, they were all fictional, and maybe more than a little idealistic. But they offered me a template to follow. More important, they gave me hope.

I was 18 when I started dating my boyfriend, Elijah.[*] The story of how we met starts like so: I wanted to write about getting a fake ID for a blog post. My roommate had met a boy named Elijah during Casino Night, and Elijah knew where to get fake IDs. So I texted him and introduced myself. Although we texted back and forth for the next few weeks, and Elijah invited me over, we didn't meet. I was busy, and, admittedly, I was nervous to go alone—what did this guy look like? What did he sound like? His dorm was full of athletes; would he be an obnoxious jock? One day, I searched for his profile on Facebook, but I wasn't impressed: Gawky middle-school photos didn't help predict the type of person he was now, and the lack of posts on his wall didn't help me assess his interests or online personality.

We didn't meet until a Halloween party, when I saw a boy dancing in the middle of the room. I tapped his shoulder and asked if he was Elijah. He turned around and shouted over the music, "I am. Who are you?"

"U-pas-na!" I said, sounding out my name. "We used to text about fake IDs."

Elijah's eyes grew wide, and he threw his arms around me. "HEYYYY!"

From then on, we were pretty much inseparable.

[*] Name has been changed.

Being with Elijah felt effortless. He was a good listener and a good conversationalist, and we enjoyed discussing politics or dissecting our favorite Kid Cudi lyrics. His laid-back personality balanced my outgoing one, and we rarely argued. Our first kiss was perfect, without any of the awkwardness I'd embraced in my books. We were best friends and lovers, but it didn't take, like, seven years. One of my friends even said, "You and Elijah are just so good at being in a relationship."

My time had come! Here I was, with all the components of an idealistic love I'd created when I was young. I basked in it. But inside, I also felt nervous: Did we fall in love *too* easily? Where was the struggle? In all the romantic comedies I've watched and young-adult books I've read, there was *also* always an obstacle between two lovers and their journey toward being together. We did not have that. And it often made me question the validity of our "love."

That summer, I was living in Chicago for an internship. Elijah drove six hours from his hometown to spend the Fourth of July weekend with me. We had four days without limits on our time; we didn't have to work around classes or studying or our friends' schedules. We could go anywhere we wanted, do anything we wanted. It was just us. Out from the bubble of our college lives—and spending time together nonstop—we learned more habits, "quirks" (too often he forgot to brush his teeth, and too often I'd go off on exhaustive, exhausting rants), and personality traits about the other. It was almost like I was dating someone new, or a different (and awfully real) version of Elijah. To be honest, I got frightened. That weekend, and its flash of reality, was like a sneak peek into the rest of our lives. And it seemed endless.

B.J. Novak has a short story, "Sophia," named after the sex-robot protagonist that falls in love with the narrator, who doesn't love her back. I was really drawn to Sophia's view of love: she tells the narrator that things in life—such as the number of taxi drivers one meets, or doctors, or nurses, and so on—are finite to her. She can count and comprehend all of them, but since humans can't, they *perceive* a lot of things as infinite (do you remember the number of cars you've seen in your life?). As a robot, Sophia can clearly see love is infinite—the only thing she couldn't calculate—and yet to humans, love is a definite structure, because we always remember the last time it ended.

I loved this idea of infinite love, and I felt it, too. When you're in love, everything expands. Even a second feels like forever. You can be sad and in love, angry and in love, disappointed and in love—there is room for so many feelings.

Being with Elijah in Chicago helped evolve my idea of love. I finally saw it as more than a two-dimensional dream (however fantastic) that involved two people and some kissing. My experience was also a contrast to what I witnessed my mother go through in her first and second marriages. At the same time, the perceived infiniteness of my relationship with Elijah made me nervous. Infinity between us felt like we had no room to evolve. We were both so young, just having finished our first year of college. Our infinite love sprang from the people we were when we met, but it wouldn't grow for the people we were becoming. I was in love and disquieted, I was in love and afraid, and one day, I wasn't in love at all. The idea of being with someone and not feeling like I had room to grow within the relationship and as my own person was an adult and scary thing to face. Suddenly, the infiniteness I was feeling was no longer a romantic idea but a horrific, never-ending nightmare.

I ended my relationship with Elijah six months after his visit to Chicago, and in doing so, felt an enormous amount of relief from the weight of infiniteness upon my shoulders. It's funny that ending something I had waited my whole life for felt *good*. My need for finding love came with expectations of the process, and the ways I wanted to feel while in love, and Elijah was not a match for those emotions. But he helped me become more confident in myself, and in how I felt. Though I still want love so badly, I can acknowledge that the desire to have feelings for someone isn't as important as *how* I feel about someone. And even if the romance ends, it's OK, because any love still offers a taste of the infinite. Now, I welcome the unknown.

OMG, YAY!

WHEN YOU WOULDA BEEN LATE, BUT THE TRAIN COMES RIGHT AWAY

↑ Exit
Knick

AND WHEN BUS DRIVERS GUN IT THROUGH EACH YELLOW LIGHT,

YES!!! YES! GO!!

MA'AM PLEASE TAKE A SEAT

420

WHEN YOU'RE SHORT ON CHANGE BUT THEY LET YOU NOT-PAY

WAAAHH..

SIGH

NEXT TIME...

OR WHEN YOU'RE CERTAIN YOU' FAILED, BUT YOU GOT IT ALL RIGH

A+

?

WHEN PUPPIES OR KITTENS SNOOZE IN YOUR LAP,

OR YOUR NEW BABY COUSIN FALLS ASLEEP ON YOUR CHEST,

SOFT Z

WHEN YOU GET MOSTLY REDS IN YOUR SKITTLES PA

...THE PART IN 'THE BALLAD OF JOHN
...D YOKO' WHEN THE MARACAS COME
...AND IT'S ALWAYS JUST THE BEST!

YOU FIND 20 BUCKS WHEN
YOU THOUGHT YOU WERE BROKE,

...R RE-DISCOVER A SNACK
...EFT FROM THE OTHER DAY,

OR WHEN THE WHOLE CLASS
LAUGHS AT YOUR SILLY JOKE,

PHEW...

TEE-HEE!

LOL!

HA HA HA

ALL OF LIFE'S LITTLE JOYS GOT ME LIKE OMG, YAY!

(*WINNER)

CLICK!

AGAINST LOVE STORIES

An ode to the failure of intimacy.

By Sally Wen Mao

I

The word *identity* has many twins. Synonyms for identity: individuality, oneness, unity, integrity, self. Other ways of seeing identity: as *absolute relation*. Identity implies default position, rootedness, orientation. Identity affirms a common experience, common blood.

The word *identity* also has opposites. The last book that the French philosopher Emmanuel Levinas published before his death in 1995 is *Alterity and Transcendence*, where transcendence is defined as the moral praxis of going beyond the self, and alterity is the paradox of the other. *Alterity* implies disorientation, alienness, the condition of exile. Alterity: alternate, other. When someone sees herself as an exile, how can she reconcile identity or "absolute relation"?

Edward Said begins his essay "Reflections on Exile" with: "Exile is strangely compelling to think about but terrible to experience. It is the unhealable rift forced between a human being and a native place, between the self and its true home: its essential sadness can never be surmounted." Exile extends beyond native place—exile has to do with the body, and the body's context and position, how the body moves in space.

Exile is the condition of alterity—to be an outcast within a culture, nation, society, community, family, partnership. To be in exile means to see the world from the vantage point of the other—

gazing from a lonely and windless rooftop, scanning for a place to call home. Like a sparrow without its migratory compass. Exile is desperate isolation and longing, and the sustained unfulfillment of that longing, the sustained failure of intimacy. Indeed, it is terrible to experience. Indeed, it is sometimes unhealable.

II

In childhood, we are haunted by white kisses, and that is the origin of our exile. We bury them in the forests where we attempt to self-preserve but they always waft out, drift back into our skins. Our bones, illuminated by the white heat of our dreams, the brown bile in our organs. Rub out the jaundice, rub out the hair, the blemishes, the phenotypes.

In our gardens of alterity, we see ourselves as the phantoms, the shells, the figments. We hunt for kisses of unknowable ghosts. We are the children of parents who were born into mass famines and wars. Mother and father shipped to the countryside, the tea fields, the rice fields. Mother and father toiling each sunrise, eating cabbage and rice, going hungry by sundown. Mother and father making a long migration. We are the children or descendents of refugees, exiles, émigrés, and immigrants who have long lost their physical homes. The earth has witnessed their partings; the earth has witnessed their estrangements and their centuries-long silences.

III

White girls kissing, being kissed. White girls, smiling with white teeth, wearing white tulle, posing in white hallways. White girls, bright like lightning. White girls at the center of love triangles, polygons, hexagons. White girls, accepting Oscars and Grammys. White girls, their plenitude of devotion. White girls falling in love, finding themselves, running through towns and cities, fast and elusive, nourished. White girls, endangered, white girls, missing, the search parties, the news reports, the sirens.

We don't question where these white girls belong. Her superficial defects can be corrected, and there are so many ways to correct them. She may have a pair of glasses, a pimple, a tattoo, but there is always room for transformation. She can transform into a geisha with a kimono in the pages of *Vogue*. She can transform into a Native American with a headdress on the Victoria's Secret runway. She has endless permutations. Her transformation is a teenage dream, where kisses are guaranteed, kisses are inevitable. Kissed, a girl is seen. Kissed, a girl is worthy. Fed by fiction and films alike that the only true path toward self-actualization is being recognized as desirable. Then loved, then possessed. This demon is male and he possesses the women he adores. Women's identities are fraught this way. That, too, is violent.

IV

The girl was born next to a famous river on the other side of the world, at the juncture of winter and spring, mid-March, Friday the 13th. The river is the Yangtse, the city is Wuhan. She is Chinese American. Her parents immigrated in the early '90s: first her father, in 1991, then her mother and her, in 1992. She spent the first seven months in America completely silent, and silence and language too were forms of exile.

The girl waited her whole life to be kissed, only to discover that a kiss is not the antidote to exile. She learned this when she turned 20. Her first kiss, in the piano room of her dormitory at the intersection of Fifth and Morewood. The boy played a song by Bob Dylan on the piano, his fingers sliding down her skirt. It was the last week of March, the vernal equinox. The striped cotton rode up his stomach when he lay her down, when he slipped his tongue between her teeth. That pale stretch of flesh.

Pittsburgh, city of rivers and steel bridges, bike paths snaking through hills. It took all her leg muscles to ride up those hills, especially the hill on Liberty Avenue that led to the Point, a meeting of three rivers: Monongahela, Allegheny, and Ohio. In her poetry class with Yona Harvey, she read a poem by Spencer Reece about spring. Then another poem by Kazuko Shiraishi in *Seasons of Sacred Lust* (1978) describing April as the "season of the sacred sex maniac."

She thought of a time, between spring and summer, a massacre following a hunger strike. She drafted a poem about heartsickness, its eternal spring. The sour gooseberry pickled in the oil of memories. A kiss is not a solution to alterity. It is not an answer, a salve—nor salvation.

V

The film *Summer Palace,* directed by the Sixth Generation filmmaker Lou Ye, follows a young woman as she migrates to Beijing for university and falls in love with another young student. They walk together under cherry blossoms, ride bikes at the edge of the lake next to the Summer Palace. The film was banned in China because it was submitted and shown at the Cannes Film Festival without the government's permission. *Summer Palace* was controversial for not only its graphic sexuality and full-frontal nude scenes, but also its depictions of the mass terror of Tiananmen Square in the spring of 1989. The camera moves frenetically as the shots are fired, the betrayal of the government occurring simultaneously with the betrayal of the protagonist's lover, who has sex with her best friend. The young lovers are torn apart, live separate lives in a fog, and 20 years later meet again, each having dreamt about the reunion for years, each having lost hope in all political matters, including the possibility of revolution and change. They are drifters, in permanent exile from hope. The man had moved to Berlin, the woman had moved to Wuhan. They book a hotel room where their lips meet for a moment, then the woman turns away, says she will buy liquor. She never returns to the room. In the morning, the man drives out and passes the woman walking by the side of the highway. This is the failure of intimacy, a failed love story.

VI

The failure to be loved, as a woman, is a kind of exile, a banishment, in itself. It's an exile from a fundamental form of belonging—the family unit, romantic intimacy. For women, failed love denotes a failure of self. A fata morgana in the distance, a flicker of pink lightning.

On the island of Tobago in spring, **the girl** watched a leatherback sea turtle dig into a mound in the sandbar. Turtle watchers combing the island for these young mothers shone a tiny red light onto the makeshift nest. A crowd of people looked on as one by one, her eggs dropped into the nest, perfectly spherical, luminous like planets.

These mothers swim thousands of miles alone to lay eggs on land, while the male turtles stay in the ocean all their lives. She usually chooses a moonlit beach. Turtles stay fertile for more than half a century. This particular turtle was 35 years old—after she laid the eggs, she would rest and then set back into the sea. The eggs would hatch without their mother.

On her way to the turtle, **the girl** in the backseat of a car with her friend, the poet Cathy Linh Che, and two tour guides from Tobago, who were driving them to the beach where the turtles were rumored to nest. An indescribable feeling thundered through her, so strong she rolled down the window and wept into the tropical wind that halved her face, again and again, hoping no one else in the car would notice.

VII

Researching for her second book of poems, **the girl** becomes obsessed with the fates of tragic women. She collects their lives and stories in an inventory. Their voices seep into her poetry—they haunt her, they comfort her, they nourish her, they keep her company on all her sad nights, this procession of gorgeous ghosts. A dead squad, if you will.

They wander on the highways by the ocean—the fictional girl on the side of the road, watching her lover speed away. Their aloneness, their eternal isolation, is what draws her to them—a troupe of faraway women, their stories in the wind.

VIII

Anna May Wong, born in 1905 on Flower Street in downtown Los Angeles, a few blocks from where the Chinese Massacre of 1871 occurred three decades earlier. The first Asian American Hollywood actress. Among the ways her characters met their fates: stabbed, shot, murdered, drowned, crushed in the 1906 earthquake in San Francisco. Her characters were abandoned by their lovers, corrupted, shunned, shamed, vilified. Her characters were never safe.

In real life, too, Anna May Wong was the empress of the lovelorn Asian woman, unmarried and single for most of her life. In the age of anti-miscegenation laws, her real lovers abandoned her as her onscreen lovers did.

According to the *New York Herald Tribune,* in 1936, during her only trip to China, she was asked if she had any romantic plans. Her answer was, "No, I expect to be wedded to my art." The next day, per the *Herald Tribune*, an English-language newspaper in Kobe, Japan, published an article that Wong planned to marry a man whose first name was Art.

IX

Graham Russell Gao Hodges wrote a biography titled *Anna May Wong: From Laundryman's Daughter to Hollywood Legend.* The acknowledgments page begins, "I first encountered the mystique of Anna May Wong on Cecil Court off Charing Cross Road in London in the fall of 1999. There, I noticed in a bookstore window an autographed photograph for sale of a beautiful woman." It is a glaring moment of alterity, the word "mystique" ascribed to an Asian American actress. If this biography were about Audrey Hepburn, surely "mystique" wouldn't be used. Mystique implies otherness, mystery, enigma, a veil of secrets.

Once in New York City, **the girl** met Hodges after he delivered a lecture at the CUNY Graduate Center. A group of people surrounded him, all eager to talk about Anna May Wong, about whom he had become an authority. She called him out for using the word "mystique." Hodge's friend, another older white man, defended his diction choice. "Isn't it true that she maybe *wanted* to be seen that way?" he remarked, chewing on his kimchi and smiling.

X

A poem by John Yau, "No One Ever Tried to Kiss Anna May Wong" (1989), begins with "She's trying to . . . turn her cup / upside down."

A poem by Jessica Hagedorn, "The Death of Anna May Wong" (1971), ends with "And I know / I can't go home again."

XI

Ruan Lingyu, actress, born in 1910 in Shanghai. Died in 1935 in Shanghai.

Chika Sagawa, modernist poet, born in 1911 in Hokkaido. Died in 1936 in Tokyo.

Theresa Hak Kyung Cha, artist and writer, born in 1951 in Busan. Died in 1982 in New York.

Iris Chang, journalist and writer, born in 1968 in Princeton. Died in 2004 in Los Gatos.

Qiu Miaojin, novelist, born in 1969 in Changhua County. Died in 1995 in Paris.

Daul Kim, model, born in 1989 in Seoul. Died in 2009 in Paris.

XII

One evening **the girl** went to a screening of Theresa Hak Kyung Cha's video works at the Museum of Arts and Design at Columbus Circle in New York. It was January, the weekend after the first snow of 2017. A grainy video of Cha's face, blinking on the screen a hundred times, the back of her head, the one frame of another face, a stranger's face. Cha, digging a mound of earth. A tree, marled. The edge of pearlescent ice and water. Cha's hands, caressing the dirt, purifying it. Her long hair reaching her knees. A railway station in South Korea, from her unfinished film, *White Dust from Mongolia.* An excerpt of a poem from EXILEE AND TEMPS MORTS:

NO NAME
NONE OTHER
NONE OTHER THAN GIVEN

XIII

If for an exile love can only be true as longing or alienation, **the girl** also sought shelter in women who have forsaken their love stories. For hurt is also, if not more, divine. Lady Chang'e, the moon goddess, lights up the night sky with her heartbreak. A hinterland of romance—famish the exiles, then banish them there.

Robyn Rihanna Fenty was the recording artist that defined her 20s. Rihanna was a prism through which all loves stretched outwardly and bent back toward self-love. Rihanna was one of the only portraits of self-affirmation—a single woman creating an empire. Rihanna's 2016 album, *Anti,* with a child on the cover, crown covering her face. It is a mask, an antidote, against the norm, against the tide, against what's expected. *Anti* is a story about alterity and survival in the wake of heartbreak and failed love stories. Rihanna, in many of her songs, likened heartbreak to "murder." So many seasons of murders.

XIV

Sadako from *Ring* is a failed love story. She is alterity incarnate, with a curtain of black hair covering her face, a threat to all social orders. In order to turn Sadako into an icon of alterity, any hope of assimilation into society must be destroyed early in her childhood.

In Koji Suzuki's original novel *Ring*, Sadako is a clairvoyant child who predicted the volcanic eruption of Mount Mihara in 1957, and whose beautiful mother committed suicide when Sadako was still young. In the story, she has no voice—she is only a rumor, spoken from the mouths of men who knew her from a distance. One man described an episode where he caught her staring into the blank screen of an unplugged television with "a faint smile on her lips." She is described as "that creepy girl," and the protagonist, Yoshino, imagined a "grotesque figure of a woman." When Yoshino finally does see a picture of her, he is confused because she is actually quite beautiful—slender, feminine, lovely, though she "lacked a certain womanly roundness."

XV

In 1999, when **the girl** was 12, her teachers removed her from her social-studies class so she could participate in a city-funded project called "The Bridges Project: A Portrait of a Community of Memories." With her other Chinese friend, she interviewed older immigrant members of the community. They learned about the history of the Chinese in San Francisco: a history of discrimination and exclusion and government-sanctioned disenfranchisement. Anti-miscegenation law was a systemic, government-sanctioned failure of intimacy, on a massive scale. **The girl** and her friend were removed from their class to learn this history. The rest of the class did not learn it.

With a group of other Chinese students chosen for the project, **the girl** and her friend traveled on a bus north to Angel Island's North Garrison, the site of the former immigration station. That day, the wind was strong—it whipped salt into their nostrils. The Monterey cypresses cast shadows over their faces. The museum simulated the original immigration detention center—its bunk beds, toilets, and facilities. A mannequin of a dejected woman on a bunk bed haunted her for years.

XVI

On Angel Island, wives were separated from husbands for months, quartered with the children in the Administration Building. Like the men in the next building, the women of Angel Island must have carved poems into the walls, poems poured forth from deep suffering. In 1940, a fire destroyed the entire building. The poems written by the men in the next building survived, but the women's poems were incinerated, silenced in the fire.

According to the anthology *Island: Poetry and History of Chinese Immigrants on Angel Island, 1910–1940*, by Him Mark Lai, Genny Lim, and Judy Yung, the lavatory of the Administration Building was haunted. No one dared to go to the restroom alone, or at night. They were afraid of the ghosts of the women who committed suicide. One of them failed the immigration examinations and jumped from the balcony. One of them hanged herself. One of them stuck chopsticks through her skull when she couldn't bear the confinement any longer. Their ghosts wandered through the bathrooms.

XVII

A Kundiman is a Filipino love song, roughly translated from

Tagalog as "if it were not so" or "if it were only." The phrase implies longing, separation, or silence. An unrequited love song. Written in the colonial regimes of Spanish and American conquest, a Kundiman is a radical love song celebrating self-preservation. It is the name of the Asian American poetry collective, one of the few communities **the girl** belongs to. Where in the world can we find radical love?

How has the idea of love become a source of suffering and trauma? According to bell hooks in her book *Communion: The Female Search for Love,* "Our obsessions about love begin not with the first crush or the first fall. They begin with that first recognition that females matter less than males, that no matter how good we are, in the eyes of a patriarchal universe we are never quite good enough." To be in love in the sense we know— the love that only exists within the boundaries of patriarchy— means domesticity and subjugation, not freedom.

Poetry is alterity in the form of language. Poetry is alterity that holds a mirror to the dream in which there is full love. She has never written a love poem. Only the aubade, the Kundiman, the parting song. She has to adapt to wildness the way a flightless bird adapts to the ground, and over time, conquers it.

XVIII

Her mother is a survivor of sarcoma, a rare blood cancer, divorce, and the Cultural Revolution. Her mother is alone now, 20 years since her divorce, and said marriage was her biggest regret. Yet her mother still urges her to get married. It's the only way she can survive on poetry, mother insists.

7:02 AM, February 2017. Mother is about to be evicted from her home, a tiny Los Altos flat she lived in for six years. Mother attempted to get rid of her belongings by calling the Salvation Army, but they refused to pick up the furniture because her flat wasn't large enough to warrant the trip.

XIX

When **the girl** was 19, she read five Murakami novels in one summer. Women always disappear in Haruki Murakami's stories. In *Sputnik Sweetheart,* the male narrator is in love with Sumire, a young aspiring novelist, and she disappears into an island in Greece. "Was the earth put here just to nourish human loneliness?" the narrator, K, asks, in despair. What these male narrators probably don't know is that being pinned under a man's gaze is *exhausting*, and Sumire escaped to Greece to avoid it. Reverence is also a form of failure, a failure to see the other person's flaws and accept them wholly, a failure of intimacy.

The girl made the initial conclusion that Sumire vanished into a fiction of her own creation, but as she grew older, she realized that, actually, Sumire had vanished into someone else's vision of her. The male imagination erases her until her very body disappears from the island of their fantasies.

XX

One summer at the Lamont Library at Harvard, **the girl** discovered a copy of *The Vertical Interrogation of Strangers* by Bhanu Kapil, a poet. A revolution of love poems about dismemberment. Her questions: "What do you remember about the earth?" "Describe a morning where you woke without fear." "Who was responsible for the suffering of your mother?"

An unnamed man was responsible for the suffering of her mother. When she was growing up, her mother would whisper about wanting to kill this man from her lab who tried to seduce her. A fissure running down the family, a fissure whose face **the girl** has never seen.

XXI

In January, it snowed in New York, and every day she climbed up the stairs of the New York Public Library, where the lions, Patience and Fortitude, guarded the petrified stone. Against all that marble, she longed for softness, sensuality—she wished for fervor, she wanted a fever to begin. She was about to turn 30. She read Audre Lorde's "Uses of the Erotic": "The erotic is a resource ... that lies in a deeply female and spiritual plane, firmly rooted in the power of our unexpressed or unrecognized feeling."

She reopened a line of communication that had been silent for a year with a former lover. She dreamt of him one night in her cold gutted apartment—he was traveling somewhere, to Greece, on a boat where the view of the Aegean Sea was deep and blue. In the dream, she felt a strong pull back toward that sea, which she touched once when she was 21.

She and her former lover were both holed up in their flats, empty with habits of isolation, separated by the Atlantic. Within a few days, she booked a flight to Berlin, where this lover lived in a flat on the last dregs of a squatter's neighborhood.

XXII

Morning, February 3rd, train in Berlin. She couldn't see the sky. About to pull into the stop. Listening to *Anti*. In the track, "Higher," Rihanna wailed in **the girl's** earbuds as she scanned the snowy train tracks. Last night she saw the Northern Lights through a porthole on the plane to Reykjavík. The flight attendants had woken the passengers so they could catch a glimpse of starry green. She never dreamt she would see them before she turned 30—the Aurora, its mythical reflection of snow.

Evening, coffee shop in Berlin. Snow crunch outside. She could not contain herself, shut herself in the bathroom where she could cry. How could she measure her own footprints here, where she was not supposed to be. Whose house will be surrounded on all sides. Who was always on the run. If she held her notebook up, he wouldn't see her. She thought about her home in Brooklyn, the lease that would inevitably expire.

The dirt in her art deco elevator, its metallic darkness. The surveillance camera inside the elevator. She was thinking about her home and how it moved without end.

XXIII

On the train to Schönfeld, she sat next to her lover. They were flying to Mallorca, Spain. From snowy Berlin to the cold heat of a Spanish island they'd never been. They could have chosen the actual Greece, Thessaloniki, which was the other cheapest flight from Berlin, but Mallorca was four degrees warmer. And four degrees made a difference.

He was not looking at her. He was focused on his screen. She had flown 3,968 miles to experience what it was like to travel to a new place with someone else—to travel somewhere not-alone, as opposed to alone. She has been to so many places by herself. She realized the feeling was more or less the same. She flipped open her book, Theresa Hak Kyung Cha's *Dictee*:

"Not a single word allowed to utter until the last station, they ask to check the baggage. You open your mouth half way. Near tears, nearly saying, I know you I know you, I have waited to see you for this long this long."

At that moment of recognition, when the poem could match the contours of her feelings, all composure fell apart. There on the train, she lost it, her eyes wet. She made wild eye contact with strangers but not him. She pulled her hat over her face, choked the dark wet bruised thing back down into her throat, inside her body where it was safe.

XXIV

Ren Hang, photographer and poet, born in 1987 in Jilin. Died in February 2017 in Beijing. Among his works accessible in the New York Public Library, two books of photographs, called *New Love* and *Athens Love*. In the books, beautiful strangers, friends of Ren's, pose naked in cattails, on the rooftops of

New York or Beijing, in the snow, in the cacti, in the fields of yellow flowers.

Athens Love chronicles a trip Ren Hang made to Greece, a beautiful, lush, sun-drenched book whose landscapes contrasted the ones in New York and Beijing in *New Love*. In one photograph, a woman lies down on an empty road naked, surrounded by lush green vegetation and a cerulean blue sky. The photograph is moving in the way the woman is positioned: lying supine, she smokes a cigarette with her eyes closed in ecstatic insouciance. Her body halves the road, which is pristine. She looks completely unaware that she is on a hot asphalt road: For all she knew, the road was her hammock. The road looks like it has never been traveled before. Her body obstructing the journey to somewhere unknown. She knows she will be OK. Even though we don't know where the road goes, it is surrounded by these beautiful green things, so perhaps we'll be OK.

XXV

The failure of intimacy, ten thousand ways. A hand stroking the thigh, a hand caressing the skin. The hand belonging to an enemy. The desire to treat the enemy with unnatural and brazen tenderness.

Is belonging the antidote to alterity? Is belonging the antidote to longing? Once living in the dead cold of Ithaca, she wrote a haiku:

> Let's take our longing
> Subtract it from belonging
> And learn to just be

Mathematics has always scared her. The formula:

BELONGING - LONGING = BE

But if this is a true formula, then:

BE + LONGING = BELONGING

XXVI

On the last night in Berlin, he woke her up in the middle of the night and held her so tightly and for so long she wondered if she was dreaming of an island in Greece again. In the morning he embraced her again and asked, "Can't you change your flight?" She couldn't. She couldn't say anything, much less stay. She had never been held that way before. It made her weep many times in the coming nights when she returned to her apartment in Brooklyn.

One week later, she attended a poetry reading at Housing Works Bookstore. By then, she and her lover had stopped their conversations. She asked the poet Ocean Vuong what she could do to appease heartache. Ocean answered: "Tame the lion only when the lion meets you. Do not seek out the beast, in order to practice your craft—or you shall be killed."

XXVII

When **the girl** was in high school, she came up with a final thesis for her Honors English class. An ecstatic declaration: "Love is a disease."

Her examples: Adam from Steinbeck's *East of Eden,* Jay Gatsby, and the women in García Márquez's *One Hundred Years of Solitude.* She cited the symptoms of love that gripped the bodies of fictional characters, the toll on their health. Spring always felt like open sores. Rebeca and Amaranta from *One Hundred Years of Solitude,* on their knees in the garden, eating dirt, eating snails because they were in love. Reciting this passage, **the girl** got on her knees, pantomiming the act, cupping fistfuls of air from the brown carpet of the classroom and eating, swallowing, the brown carpet where there was no love.

XXVIII

A few weeks later, the lion spoke. A hypochondriac, he was worried about his flu symptoms, his illness. He was worried that her body was contagious and contained the pathogens. She assured him she had a blood test done recently and that the results came out normal.

He assumed that she was looking for love, and said he couldn't give her what she was looking for. They then had a conversation about love that she didn't want. He believed that everyone searched for love. He believed that love was an emotion, and that she was entitled to love because she was a human, and it bothered and offended him that she was not looking for love from him, even though he couldn't give it to her.

And that, too, was a failure of intimacy: her inability to express why hunger was a given, not love. bell hooks, in *Communion: The Female Search for Love,* writes, "This is a female's first lesson in the school of patriarchal thinking and values. She must earn love. She is not entitled. She must be good to be loved. And good is always defined by someone else, someone on the outside."

XXIX

The failure of love is rooted in complex systems of oppression that erase the humanity of those on the margins and outskirts. When someone has been in this marginal position for a long time, love is not a given. Love is not a given for exiles. Love is not the answer in a patriarchal capitalist white supremacist universe. Love cannot exist without justice.

XXX

Then spring arrived, **the girl** turned 30, and the sun returned. Tulips planted in the flowerbeds next to the library. Regeneration like a form of sickness. In the Rose Main Reading Room, the windows open to the sun-stained buildings, the cathedrals, the glass and steel facades. She read Rilke. She read Lorca. She read Hikmet. The beauty of spring was a kind of exile, too. Shut out from the sweetness of cherry blossoms, she listened to recordings of writers, including the *New York Public Library Podcast*. In one episode, a recording of an NYPL event with Elizabeth Alexander, Hilton Als said, "When we stay open to the possibility of love and connection, that weird relaxation happens to us all. I'm ancient. It's not the youth that makes love accessible, I think it has everything to do with where we put our bodies: in the line of fire."

The girl rewound the podcast again and again to hear the words echo. In the line of fire. Her body, a wound or a petal, she couldn't say. Als goes on to say: "Everyone has to have at least one person in their lives that they tell the absolute truth to." For a long time, she thought this person, for her, was the unidentified reader she was writing to. That fall and winter, she tried to avoid every couple in sight among the swaying London plane trees of Bryant Park. She felt the quicksand sensation that love only existed for other people, not for her. And other times she was struck by the terror that love could exist, even for alterity incarnate. She wrote in her journal: "From a young age, I've been crippled by hope. Hope that someday I could belong somewhere despite the fact that I was hopelessly different. Hope that someday there will be a person I could tell the absolute truth to without being afraid."

Even if, as an exile, a connoisseur of heartbreak, she has never experienced real, radical love. Even if love meant trauma. The hope for radical love is also a choice she could make. She could choose to have hope. She could choose sickness. O, to be tender. She has lived until now without it.

DO SISTERS ACTUALLY LOVE EACH OTHER?

Insider 👀 on the Hughes sisters.

By Jazmine Hughes

Occasionally, if I'm lucky, my phone gets overturned and forgotten for a few minutes, or it's stuck in a coat pocket in a closet and out of reach, or its battery dies. When I return, I'll have dozens of texts waiting for me, all from Cheetah Sisters, the group text I share with my younger siblings. It is a free-for-all, chock full of memes and attacks and requests to "PLEASE CLOSE MY DOOR WHEN YOU EXIT MY ROOM, JERMANE" and appeals for advice and the dredges of real-life arguments and an unending stream of ugly photos of one another. Mostly, though, it's a place for our inside jokes: the manifestation of our intimacy, a language all our own.

We don't come from a close-knit family—no hugging, no crying, no lessons learned—so we just text constantly, and feel comfortable staying in touch at arm's length. We don't come from a close-knit family, yet we text constantly, and I find myself choking back laughter whenever I read the scrollback, often only contributing "SCREAMING" to the melee, trying and failing to explain a joke with 15-year-old roots to an IRL bystander. The group text has strengthened our bonds, just as it's possible that age or time or our parents' divorce or the weight of the world has made us lean in closer to one another, as sisters. Ending up with these four people is just the luck of the draw: none of us chose each other, so

251

I wanted to know if we even liked each other, if we *would* choose each other if we could. I wondered what, if anything, would make us friends.

CAST OF CHARACTERS

Jazmine: I am 25. I live in New York City.

Jermane is 23. She lives in New Haven, Connecticut, with our father. She is bossy, which is why everyone hates her, but she is often right.

Javonne is 20 and a junior at Johnson & Wales. Her twin, Javonda, lives in New Haven and is planning to move to California.

J'Mari is 18. She lives in New Haven, too.

Jessie is the dog.

JAZMINE OK! First question: Do we like each other?

I like you guys now. I still think you are all jerks.

JERMANE U alright

JAVONDA I like you all cuz I'm supposed to. But J'Mari would be that friend I talk to in class and only cuz I have nobody and I'd never talk to Jermane. Maybe only to get study guide answers or something. Javonne is the bestie and Jazmine is the cool kid I want to notice me.

JAZMINE When did you start to like everyone?

You guys all loved me when I moved out

JERMANE Once the twins graduated from high school I started to like them more

I've always liked J'Mari

JAVONDA Yeah Jazz you've always been cool. J'Mari has just been the baby so I think we secretly liked her. And Jermane has been back and forth

JERMANE I literally do nothing to you people.

JAZMINE I sort of like Jermane. She's OK.

J'MARI I like y'all

I just prefer the dog

And I've always liked y'all. But it wasn't until last year that me and Nonda became best friends

JAZMINE DID YOU GUYS KNOW THAT J'MARI AND JAVONDA ARE BEST FRIENDS

SHE TOLD ME AND I CRIED

J'MARI BEST FRIENDS!!

JAVONDA THIS IS A FORCED FRIENDSHIP I'VE BEEN TRYING TO REACH OUT FOR HELP

J'MARI She's just joking

JAZMINE Nonda, do you not want to be best friends with your little sister?

JAVONDA Nah, on some real J'Mari and I are only homies because I don't have any friends. And Jermane is mean to me.

JERMANE I'M NOT MEAN

JAVONDA 😑

JAZMINE Javonda, does J'Mari keep you less lonely?

Will you talk to her every day after you move to Cali?

Is Javonne your best friend?

J'MARI No I am.

JAVONDA Yeah J'Mari is like my new dog I bought because of a tragedy or something

I'll snap her when I'm in Cali! Maybe call to bother her or be random

But Javonne is da GOAT

JAZMINE J'Mari, are you gonna miss Nonda when she moves?

JAVONDA THE PEOPLE WANNA KNOW LAME-ARI

I feel bad tho for leaving her alone

She only has the pups

Yo we need friends :'(

J'MARI Nah I won't miss her that much I have the dog

JAVONDA :/

JAZMINE Would you guys say that you're closer to your sisters than your random friends?

J'MARI Yeeeee

JERMANE I guess but not really

JAZMINE Say more

JAVONDA Ummm yes and no. I don't tell them my business but we're always together, and I act stupid and don't have my guard up when I'm home

JERMANE ^^^^

JAZMINE Am I your friend?

JAVONDA Yeah, you're the cool sis

JERMANE Jaz, you're everyone's friend.

JAVONDA #facts

JAZMINE But am I your COOL SIS or your friend?

Because a cool big sister is sort of a one-way thing, right?

Like I don't call and tell you about my life

And friendship is a two-way street

JERMANE Yeah, you're the cool sis but we can tell you everything and you'd spit truth

JAVONDA Mmmhmm

JAZMINE I'M CRINE

THANK YOU

OK here's a question

Do you guys love each other

Even if you don't like each other

JAVONDA Um I guess we love each other

(the dog wrote that)

J'MARI Yeah I guess too

JAVONNE I came back to, like, eighty messages to read and I will not.

Someone fill me in if you want an answer from me.

JAVONDA Jazmine is interviewing us

Asking if we're all friends or just sisters pretty much

JAZMINE Yes

Are we your friends

And do you love us?

JAVONNE Um I think we're all . . . sisters

Me and Javonda are friends but sisters with everyone else. Like we're cool duh but I'm not gonna voluntarily text you all for no reason, besides Javonda.

And of course I love you all. "Blood is thicker than water." *rolls eyes* but there are mad snakes in the world and your fam is the only true blue so I have mad love for you all

(not really true but u know)

JAVONDA RT 🙏👌🔥🍕💯📝🔑

JERMANE Yeah I guess

JAZMINE I'M CRINE

Did you guys always feel this way

Or did it happen recently, after you got old and mature

JERMANE Within the past few years

Like, I never understood why mommy CALLED Auntie Sherri

JAVONNE Maturity def

JAVONDA Forreal! I never understood why she called her either but now I get it.

JAZMINE Do you guys call each other?

JAVONNE Only Nonda. So no.

JERMANE Nope.

We all live together

JAVONNE One time I wanted to text J'Mari but I forgot lol

JAVONDA I think we'll only call if it's been 10 lunar eclipses and we're super bored and wanna freak the other sister out

JAZMINE Yeah, sometimes when I call you guys to say hi you freak out

But I thought we were all besties?

Maybe you hate the phone?

JAVONDA Who hates the phone? Only Lame-ari does

JAZMINE Yeah I called her yesterday and it sucked

J'MARI :/

JAVONDA Her ratings aren't the best

You should've checked Yelp before you called her

JAZMINE Why doesn't anyone call me then?

JAVONDA You're a star. I kinda assume you're always busy or drinking wine or sobering up from drinking wine

JAZMINE What does sisterhood mean to you all?

JAVONNE Being there through the I-hate-yous and mess ups and still being sisters and having one's back and loving them and junk

JAVONDA Um that unbreakable bond through thick and thin, even though we hate each other

JERMANE Nonda came to preach!

JAVONDA U know I spit facts

JAZMINE J'Mari,

Hello

What does sisterhood mean to you?

J'MARI Having sisters.

STICK 'N' POKE

She's lost control.
By Laia Garcia

I don't think it's there anymore.

I had just gotten into bed when I realized I hadn't seen it in a while. I thought back to when I got out of the shower earlier and looked at my naked body in the mirror. Had I looked at my hips? Was anything there? When was the last time I had seen this tattoo?

I stared at the dark ceiling as I lay snug underneath my covers. Should I check if the tattoo was still there? Surely, it must be, but what if it had really disappeared?

I have never been addicted to drugs or alcohol. I have never engaged in dangerous sexual activities. I have never been a "bad girl." I have never been one to willingly lose control of myself.

I think about this often as a shortcoming. My inability to let myself lose control feels like a barrier to my fully becoming a woman. To be a woman is to lose yourself in something and to maybe come back from it triumphant. Do all the things you're not supposed to, come close to death, then relinquish the vices, write about it, become a woman.

How can I become a woman if I have no interest in becoming a cautionary tale.

On the year I turned 27 years old, I decided my life up to that point was not turning out the way I wanted. That year I broke up

259

with the boyfriend I had been dating on and off for the better part of five years. I realized that I had spent most of my adult life in two long-term relationships. I had not slept with enough people, I thought it should be at least ten (a nice number if you are thinking of embarking on a controlled experiment, which I definitely was). I joined OkCupid.

Let's see what happens if I do this thing became my mantra. I went on dates with boys I met online, I went home with boys I met in real life. I let an Argentinian break my heart. I flirted with a boy in a band while they were playing onstage. I got involved with a boy and then broke up with him despite the fact that we never once kissed or had sex for the entire three months of our "tryst." I was following my desires wherever they took me. I look back at pictures of me during this time and am happy, because I was doing exactly what I wanted and when I wanted. And then I met Joseph.*

Joseph messaged me first, and I liked him because he had used a pencil as a pickup line, which was completely ridiculous but also utterly perfect. After two weeks, we made plans to meet for dinner. I was not expecting anything to come of it. It was a Sunday night and I had work the next day. I did not shave my legs. I did not carefully pick out an outfit. I was not nervous.

Joseph was by far the most handsome man I had ever been with on a date, which did not actually make me nervous, because he was out of my reach. But then drinks turned to dinner, and by the time dessert came around we kissed after one bite of the apple tart we were sharing. We kissed on the street on the way to a bar and we kissed at the bar ignoring the drinks we had ordered while we were trying to ignore that all we wanted was really each other. We eventually made our way back to his place. I fell asleep with my head on his chest.

This was a fun night, I thought, *but there's no way this will become anything else.*

* Name has been changed.

Except I saw him the next day and the next day and the day after that. We didn't so much start dating as much as we just did not leave each other's side. He said *I love you* a few weeks in, and I remember feeling the world spinning around me. That was October.

By the following February, things were already slipping away. There were serious conversations to be had. The bubble had burst, but instead of walking away I was bathing in the sticky soapy spots on the floor.

That July we broke up. He wasn't attracted to me, he said. I was too young, he said. I was too depressed, he said. We got back together a week later, at my friend's wedding.

It was never the same after that, and now looking back there were so many times I thought I needed to get out of it. *But relationships take work*, I told myself. *This is what being an adult is like*, I told myself.

That November we broke up. He wasn't attracted to me, he said. He wanted to see other people, he said. Still, I spent Thanksgiving with him and his family. Sleeping in the same bed but not touching each other. That winter his apartment lost heat so he temporarily moved in with me. We were back together by February, but it was probably the circumstances more than anything else.

I understood our relationship had no legs to stand on. I knew I couldn't trust him. I knew I was becoming a different person. I knew I was putting up with lies and behaviors that were not OK. Things that an old version of me would've had no patience for. But this was a new me. I couldn't walk away. I didn't want to walk away.

Suddenly, I realized I had completely lost control of myself. I had been going on a years-long bender and I had developed an addiction to see how much I could feel, how many things I could put my heart and my brain through and still wake up the next day, ready for more. Although I had a lot of shame about this behavior I also felt a weird sense of pride. Pride in how much I could handle. How much I'd be willing to stand.

That month at a friend's house, the topic turned to stick 'n' poke tattoos. My friend had ink and needles, and in the ultimate junkie move, Joseph tattooed a childhood nickname of his on my hip.

Let's see what happens if I do this thing.

They say matching tattoos are bad luck for the couple, but we already had no future. There was nothing to risk, no luck to hope for. It wasn't so much a symbol of our love to each other, but a symbol of *my* unwavering commitment to love, to this love that had become lethal somewhere along the line. "Je ne regrette rien," I wrote in a journal. I had finally given up all control, I had gone mad.

That July we broke up again and got back together in the space of a couple hours. Neither ready to be without the other. I was his crutch and he was mine.

I was certain he had started seeing someone else.

I was high as a kite on emotions. Listening to Fiona Apple and Sheryl Crow songs to feel everything more. Their voices like a blade on my skin. I felt everything so much. How much deeper could I take it all.

And still I stayed.

The following April, after dinner with his brother and his brother's girlfriend at the same restaurant where we had our first date, I broke up with him. We had planned for me to spend the night at his place, but as we were getting ready to hail a cab he said he would prefer to fly solo. It was a minor detail, but it was the last straw. My life had become exhausting. There were text messages from an ex-girlfriend (*the* ex-girlfriend), and their dubious explanation. The time I went on a work trip to Europe when he sent only two or three emails in the two weeks I was away.

My limits could not be tested any further. Not by me. Not by him. The experiment was over. No one could ever say I didn't try, that I threw in the towel and walked away when things became difficult. I had turned our relationship into a trial by fire, and I was Khaleesi, being reborn. It was done.

Almost a year later, all these things came flashing back to me as I lay in bed, wondering whether the tattoo he had given me was still on my hip.

I turned over on my side, closed my eyes, and fell asleep.

I did not check to see if it was still there.

MAYBE ONE DAY

By Shania Amolik

we'll bump into each other
in the elevator of some government building
or in a crowded train
and we'll talk like we don't know who
we are,
like we don't know each other.
We'll joke about the weather and
the crazy length of my hair.
It'll be familiar,
comfortable conversation.
It'll feel like sunny Sunday mornings,
you pouring me tea in the mug
that will come to be my favorite,
me reading aloud parts of the paper I know
you'll like.
It'll seem promising
so we'll exchange phone numbers
(as if a thread of conversation between those digits doesn't
already exist on our phones)
and pencil in plans for a casual Saturday lunch date
at that café near your apartment
(as if you hadn't already taken me a thousand times to that café,
as if the waitress there hadn't had my tea order memorized)
And we'll walk away.

The elevator will have arrived
at my floor or the train at your station
But as we step away from each other,
we'll come to our senses
I'll remember
Who you are:
The boy who used to hold my heart in
his hand,
who let his fingers span out once in a while,
letting whatever rested in his palm fall
and
shatter when it hit the floor.
Who I was:
The girl who couldn't say no to you,
who wanted all you had to give
even when you didn't want to give to her.
In that moment we'll realize
Who we have become:
A boy that learnt to respect other people and
A girl that learnt to respect herself.
And we'll know that the people we are now
won't use the numbers we've just been given.

HOW TO TOUCH ME

Something resembling closeness.
By Bhanu Kapil

Perhaps it is not night. Perhaps the sky is the color of daffodils and silver coins, a sign that a great storm is about to break open along the dark blue seam that has appeared above the city. Is this a city? Perhaps it is the verge of something, the place where the pasture and little gray fields give way to the hills.* The hills are red. The mud there is a dark orange, easily compacted into balls and other round shapes, the pre-goddess forms, both male and female, that are then dried, spotted with a luminous white pigment, then carried into the river until they dissolve. Thus to "return the goddess to the goddess," a phrase that in English seems generic, like squatting in the back garden to pee when you have your period and the moon is shining through the ash trees like the end of something and the beginning of something else. I read about this in a magazine. I read that your body is made of water, fire, and earth. That you and the planet make a circuit that glitches and flows. That before you have sex you are cobalt blue, and afterward, a lighter blue, the blue of periwinkles, a June sky in Western Europe, the tongue of a lizard you once saw when you were visiting your grandmother in Chennai and she left you in the kitchen with your cup of warm milk, which had been boiled, as usual, with turmeric, ginger, and cardamom (ground into a thick paste).

* Can you imagine this scene? Let the city and then the pasture and hills soften, until, from the sky, it's just smoke and gleaming lamps,

a secondary darkness that makes every smell—burning juniper, flatbread roasting on an open fire—akin to taste. Let your body float, in a way that feels natural to you, into the red hills. There, there. Descend. This is the place.

How to touch me: Don't tell me when I wake up in the morning that you will touch my arm later tonight,** the inner part of my arm, stroking it so lightly, over and over again, from the crease of my elbow to the curve of my shoulder, so that my whole life I will associate this touch with the roaring darkness that comes down from the Shivaliks, the hills (neither red nor green) that I realize now I will never be able to describe. Don't tell me this will happen even as we eat breakfast, then lunch, with your brothers and sisters, beneath the guava tree, on the little bamboo stools that were woven by hand. Don't look at me or talk to me in anything but an ordinary way. In this way, when you touch me, the electricity in my body will flare a difficult, complex, unremitting violet, then soften. Like cream.

** When I was 15 years old, we went to India for the summer. The day our plane took off, the sky above London was like pleated tin. Then we broke through the clouds into that dazzling light, which I will never forget. A beautiful hazard: to go and keep going. Or, at least, at the age of 15, to arrive, slightly numb, not expecting anything to ever happen, not here, in the ancestral village where your mother's cousin lives. The first few days in the large, uncomfortable country house, I am overcome with loneliness and jet lag, reading then rereading *Through the Looking-Glass, and What Alice Found There*. I write poems in my little notebook with the English robin on the cover, cross-legged on the granary, a huge metal cabinet covered with a cotton bedsheet and filled with winter wheat. It is the only private place in the house, this massive metal box behind a batik curtain in the kitchen, tucked inside a tiny room. Below it is the garden, which is a vibrant, dark green: monsoon-wet, sparkling and more alive than anything I ever saw in my whole life, even the lochs of Scotland, which I visited once, to look for the monster: a leaf, an azalea, then the gleam of a cobra*** as it slips off.

*** That morning, I woke up on the jute bed, a cot really, in the garden, outside, pushing the mosquito net off my body, then sitting up to swing my legs over the side, to slip on my flip-flops. Then I saw it: the entire, intact, massive shed skin of a king cobra. During the night, the night you stroked my arm, over and over again, until my entire body was a pure block of vibration, the snake must have found its place. Beneath me. Beneath us. You were in the next cot, and I thought you were asleep. Goodnight, you said. Goodnight, I said. Then you touched me, your fingertips brushing my skin so lightly that, at first, I did not feel it. Your touch. I froze. Perhaps the first time you see an owl or a leopard, or someone dying, you don't recognize what it is: before you. A curve in the forest. Looking up, perhaps. A branch. The slowing down of the breath. A face you've never seen before, this close. How to touch me? Don't speak of this night**** ever again. When morning comes, and I scream, leaping from the cot, away from the shed skin, the skin I don't recognize as a cobra's in that first instant, only understanding it was there, meet my eyes, but with ordinary, familial concern, the same expression in the eyes of everyone who runs toward me—a mother, an aunt, a sibling— from the interior rooms. Meet my eyes without shame or curiosity. Meet my eyes as if it was a Tuesday morning, and not the morning that a snake shed its skin beneath my bed: the morning, that is, that follows night.

**** I am trying to describe the night I slept outside, as is the custom in the warmer months, in a bricked-in garden, on a cot. My mother and her cousin were inside, with the younger children, and for some reason the women had allowed him, my mother's cousin's adopted son—the son of her husband from a formermarriage whose wife had died in childbirth—to sleep next to me, in the open air, on one of the two rickety cots. Where were the men? They were pilgrims, high in the mountains, hitching rides on oxcarts to Badrinath, the place where a glacier becomes a fountain.***** Perhaps they were drinking beer or chai at a roadsidestall. Perhaps they had inverted themselves, already, above a living spring, one of the streams below the sacred site. Where were they? I simply recall that we were alone.

***** You lifted the mosquito net that covered me. Perhaps you were on your side, your left arm folded beneath your head. You were speaking, murmuring, as you began to touch me. You touched only this part of my body, the inner arm. Is this true? As I write these words, I remember your hand brushing the hair out of my eyes. I remember your fingertip tracing the new silk of my right eyebrow. I remember your lips on my wrist. I remember the stars: shattered, glottal, bursting and streaming, through the net that covered my face and body. I remember the fireflies in the garden, spitting light, and the hum of garden frogs, and the heavy sweetness of the night-blooming jasmine, raat ki rani, that grew along the wall.

And in the morning, I screamed, my feet recoiling from my makeshift slippers.

And by afternoon, I had returned to the world of Lewis Carroll.

And for the rest of the summer, I tried to catch your eye, but you never caught mine.

And when you grew up, you relocated to Dubai with your beautiful family, where you currently work in sales.

And when I grew up, I stopped feeling anything in the many parts of myself, from the various shocks I received in the process of loving, and being loved.

And yet, writing these words, I remember that night, and I feel a pulse in the part of me that is like a fin. It is like a hand.******

How to touch me?

****** Like this. Like that. Again.

ACKNOWLEDGMENTS

Thank you to . . .

Everyone who wrote something for this book, exploring every thought and feeling to their most subterranean and cosmic levels. Writing anything makes one vulnerable, writing about love makes one vulnerable, and being edited makes one vulnerable. Plus, that stuff is time consuming. Thank you for giving your time and strength to this process.

Lauren Redding, *Rookie*'s publisher, for managing this project and working so closely with Tina, Allegra, Razorbill, and me on every aspect of this book. As with all of *Rookie*, it would have been impossible without you and your unwavering commitment to our community.

Tina Lee, for editing every piece in this book with such care, helping our writers to bring their internal worlds to the outside, and helping to bring *Rookie on Love* to its full potential.

Allegra Lockstadt, for making our cover and interior artwork as beautiful as everything you do. You have always been a crucial part of *Rookie*'s visual identity and community, and we are lucky to see this anthology through your eyes.

Cynthia Merhej, for lettering the type on our cover and creating the *Rookie* logo years ago. You drew it before we had even settled on a name, but you perfectly captured the spirit of this endeavor.

Elly Malone, for lending your brilliance to the illustrations for the piece "Binary Planets."

Annie Mok, for being a multitalented visionary and creating the rad illustrations for your piece, "Living by the Blade."

Diamond Sharp, for using your keen eye to choose the poems by *Rookie* readers that were right for this book.

Derica Shields, for recommending some of the excellent contributors in this collection.

Lena Singer, for interviewing Marlo Thomas for her piece, "From Spark to Bonfire."

Ben Schrank, Jessica Almon, Marissa Grossman, Kristin Boyle, and Maggie Edkins at Razorbill for making this book a reality.

David Kuhn and Kate Mack at Kuhn Projects for fostering this project in its early stages.

Sarah Chalfant and Rebecca Nagel at Wylie Agency for helping us make the book we wanted and believing so steadfastly in *Rookie*'s vision.

Our readers, for supporting us and each other, online and in print. Thank you for creating a corner of the universe where the definition of love can be expansive and ubiquitous.